Amazing Horses
Relaxing Coloring Book

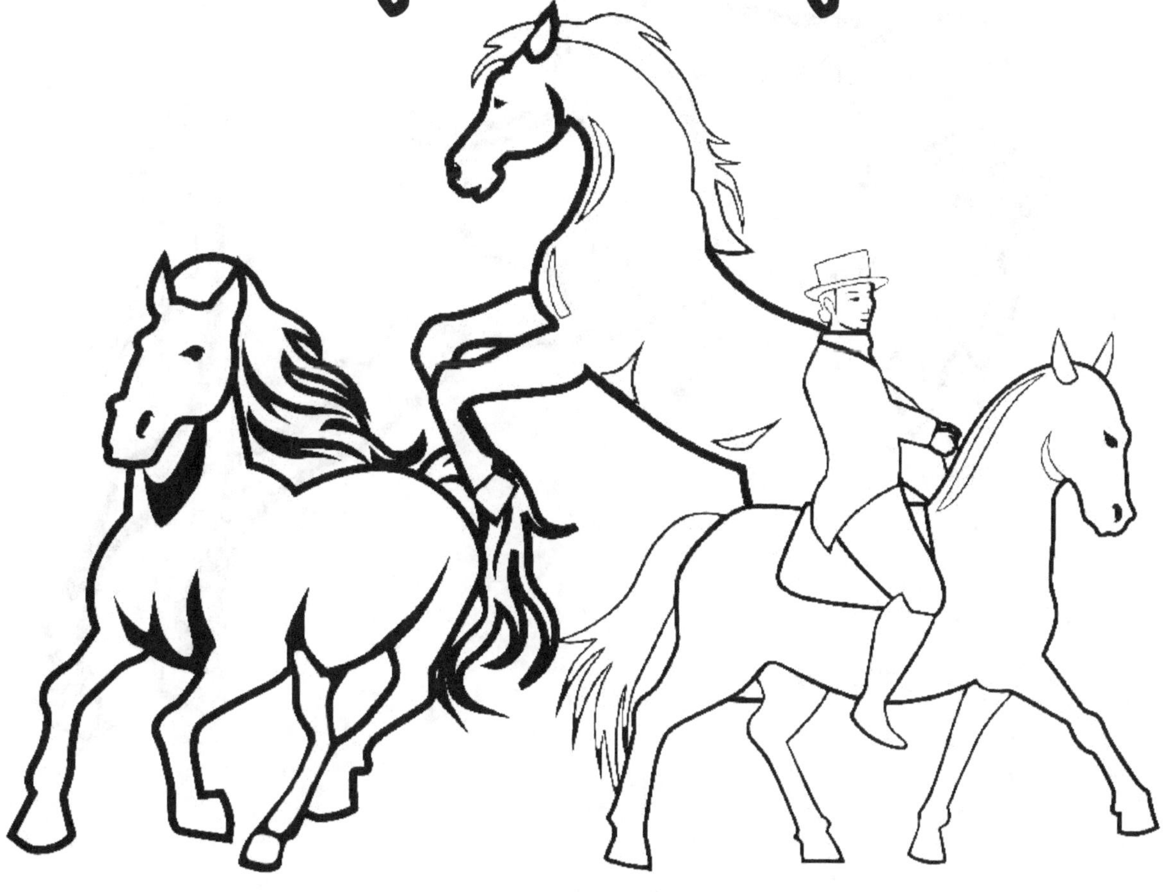

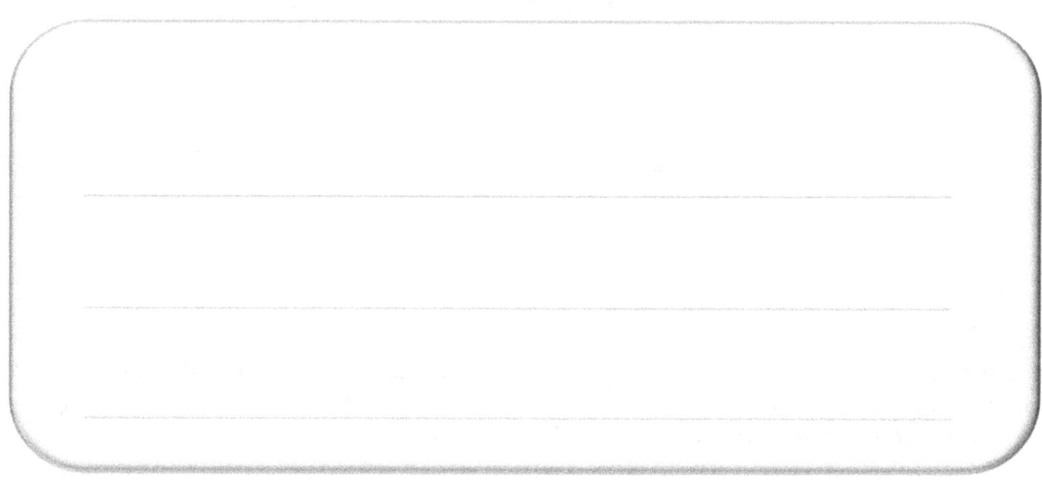

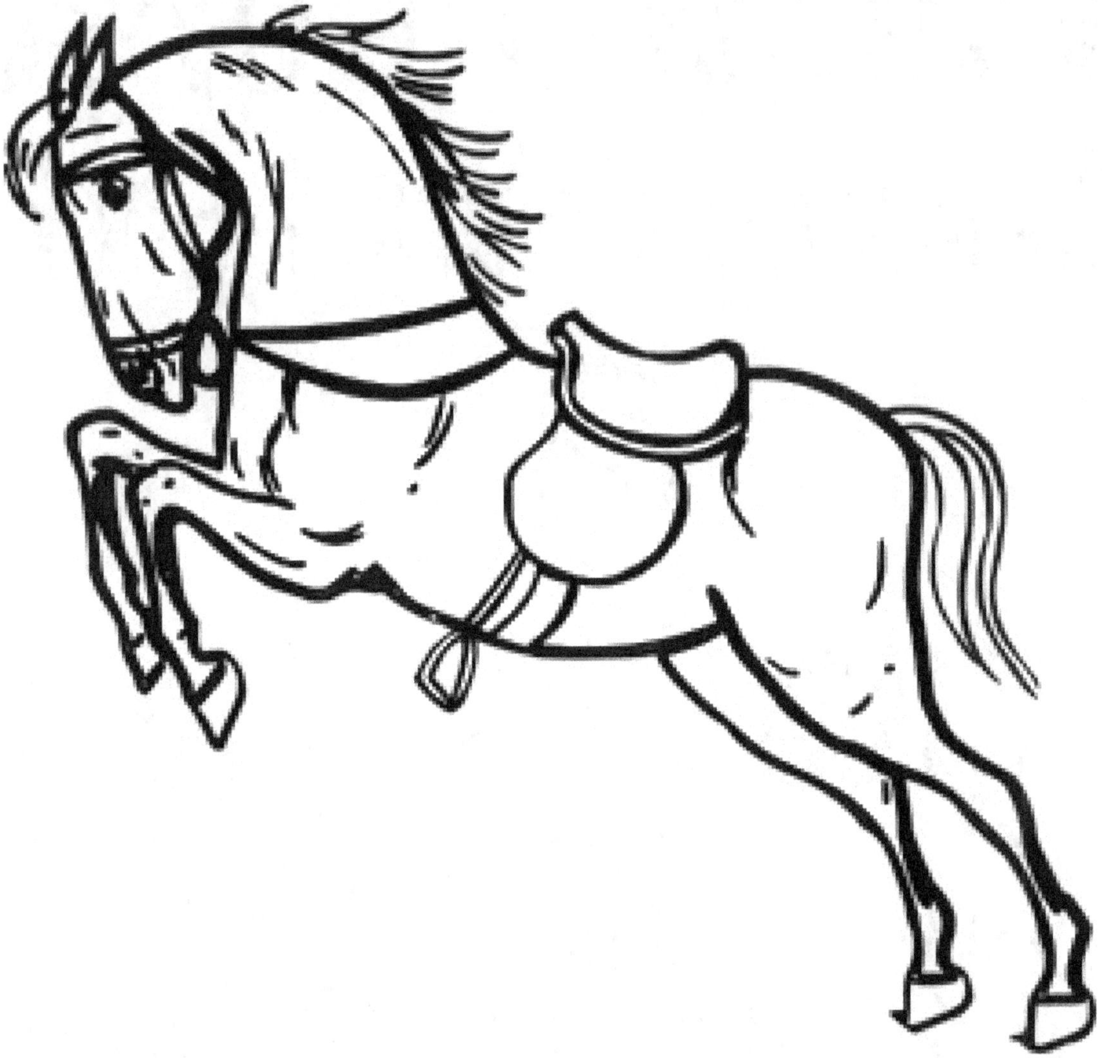

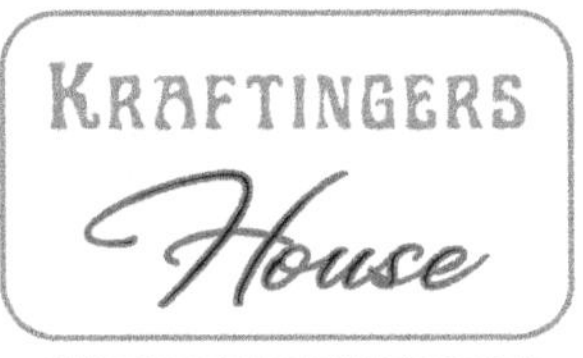

Email: targetingtriumph@gmail.com

Thank you! Please leave a review, comment, and suggestion to improve our products.

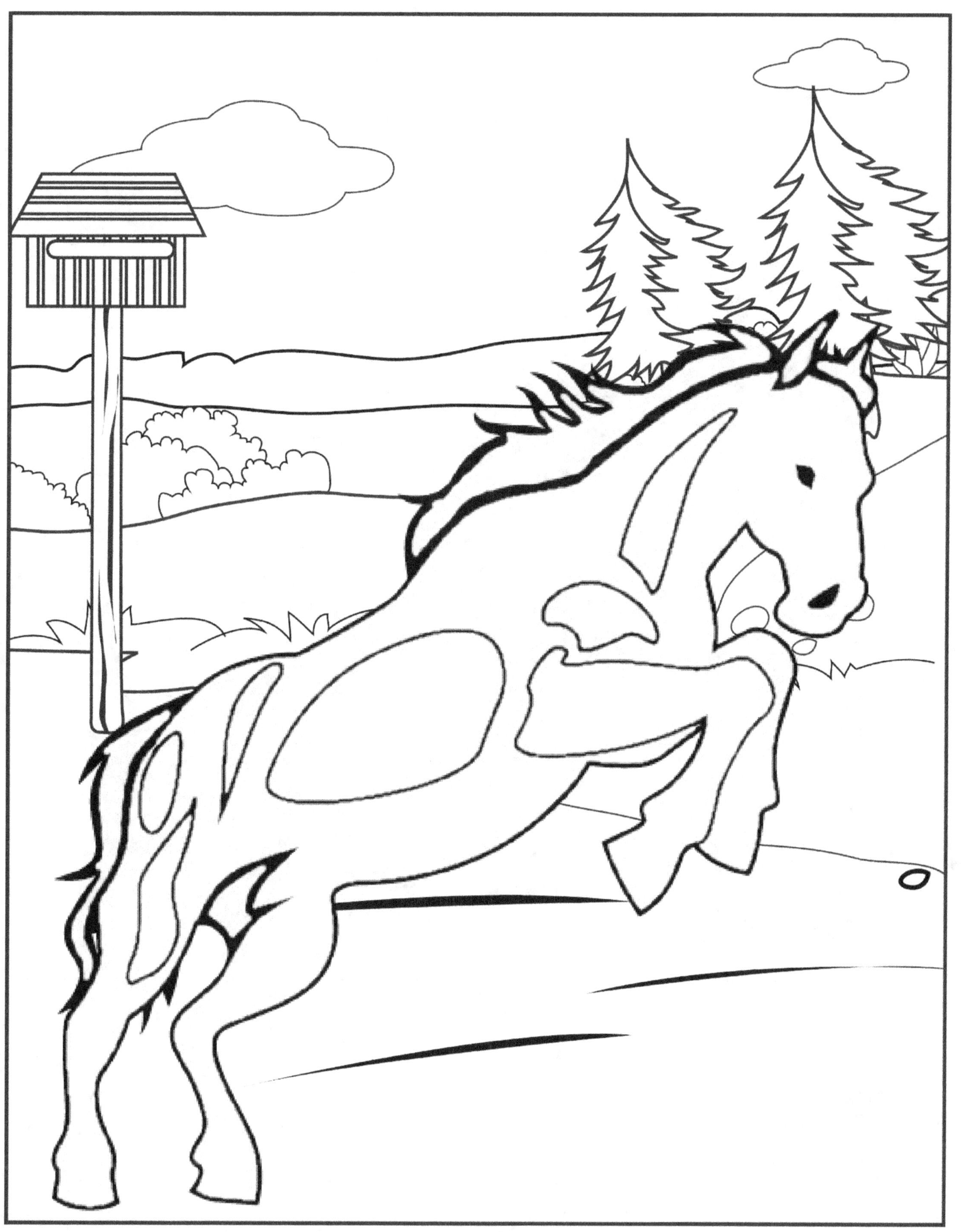

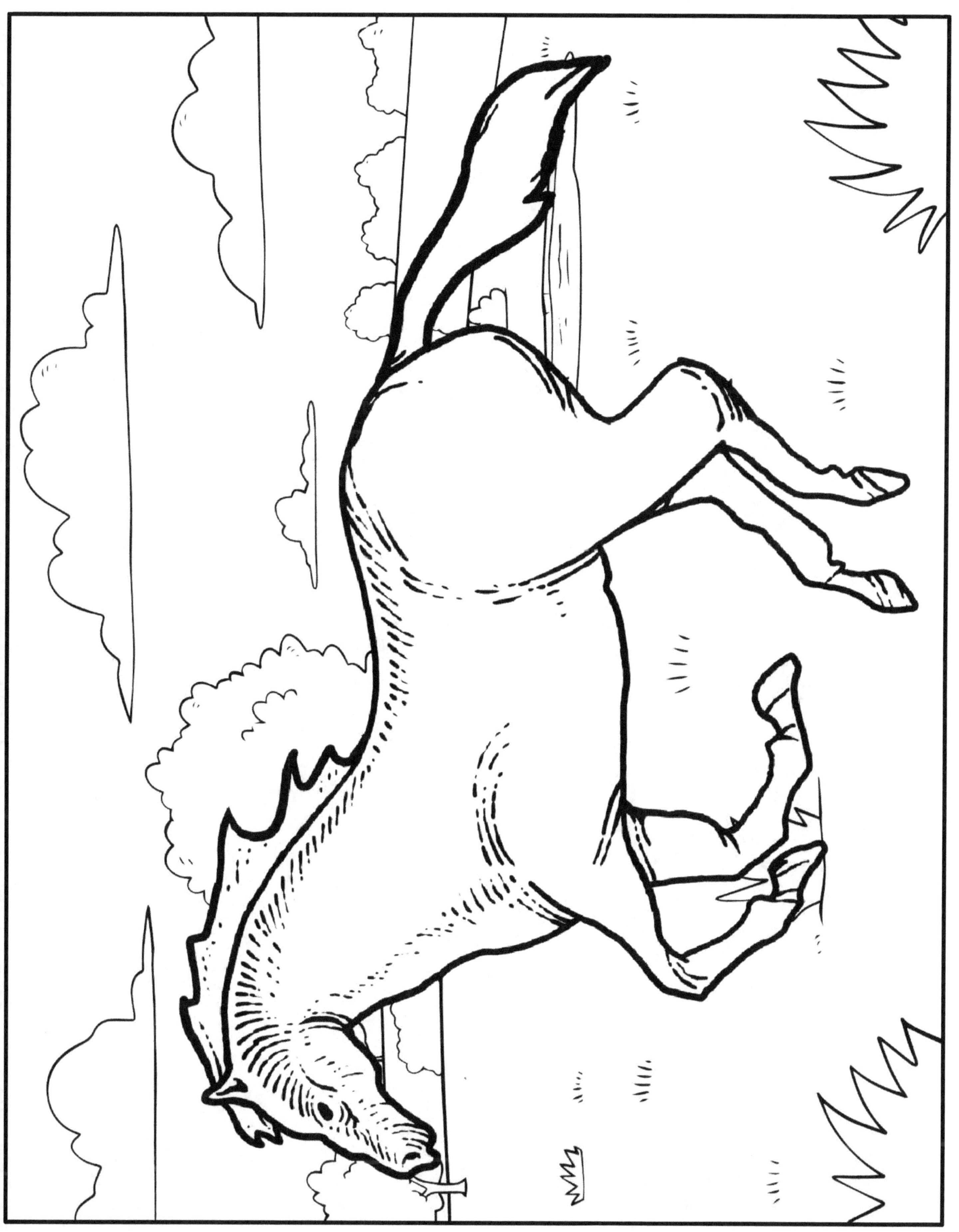

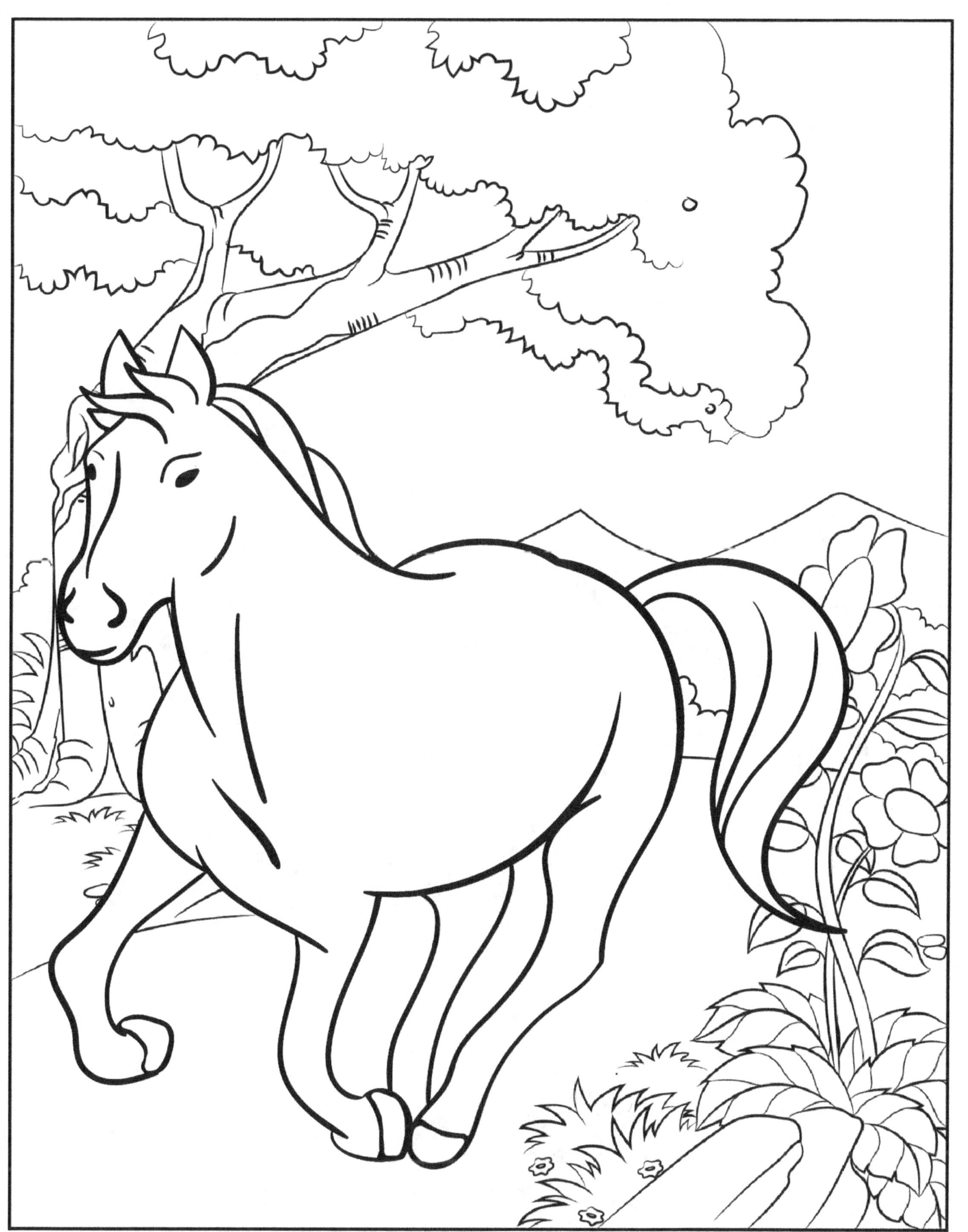

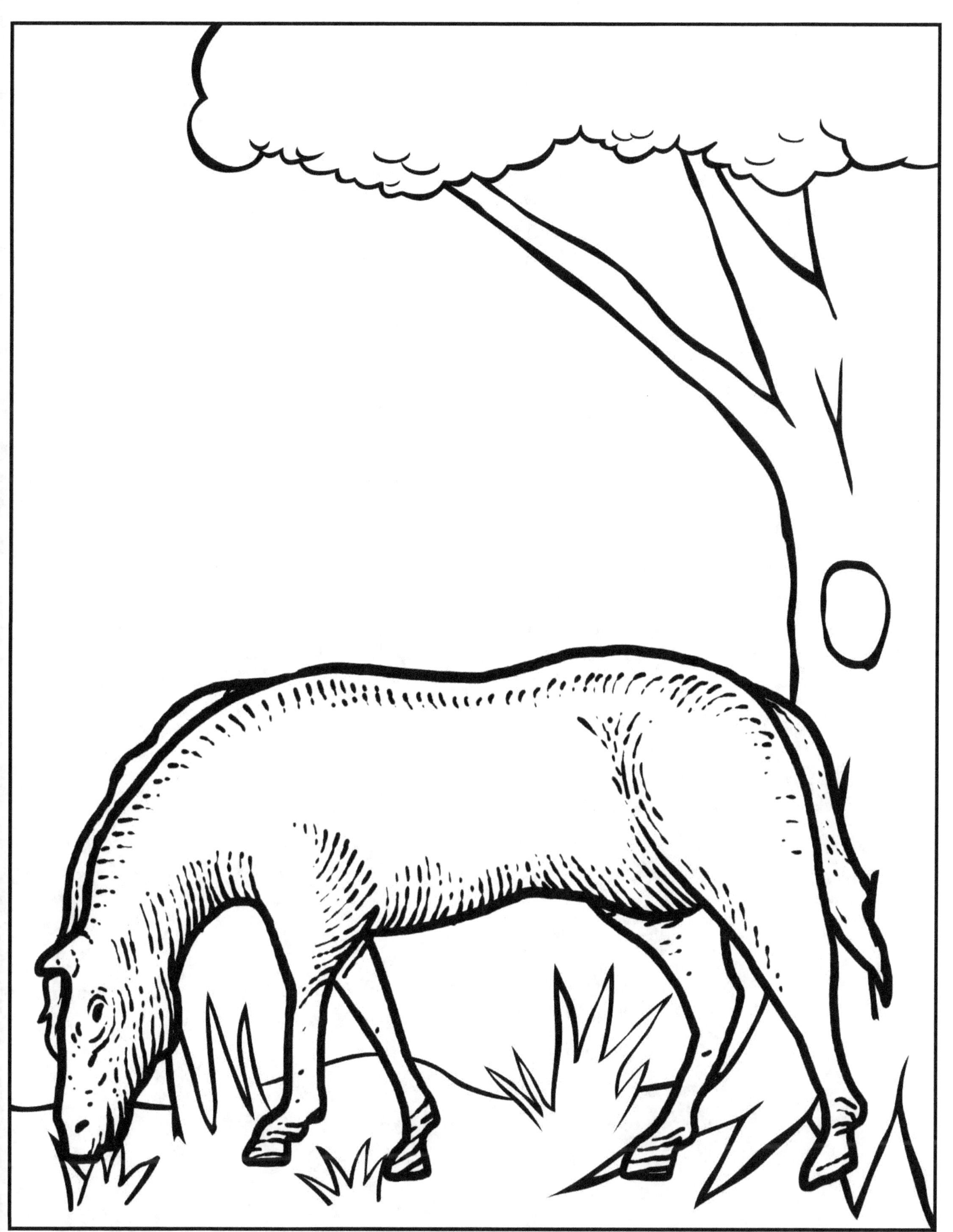

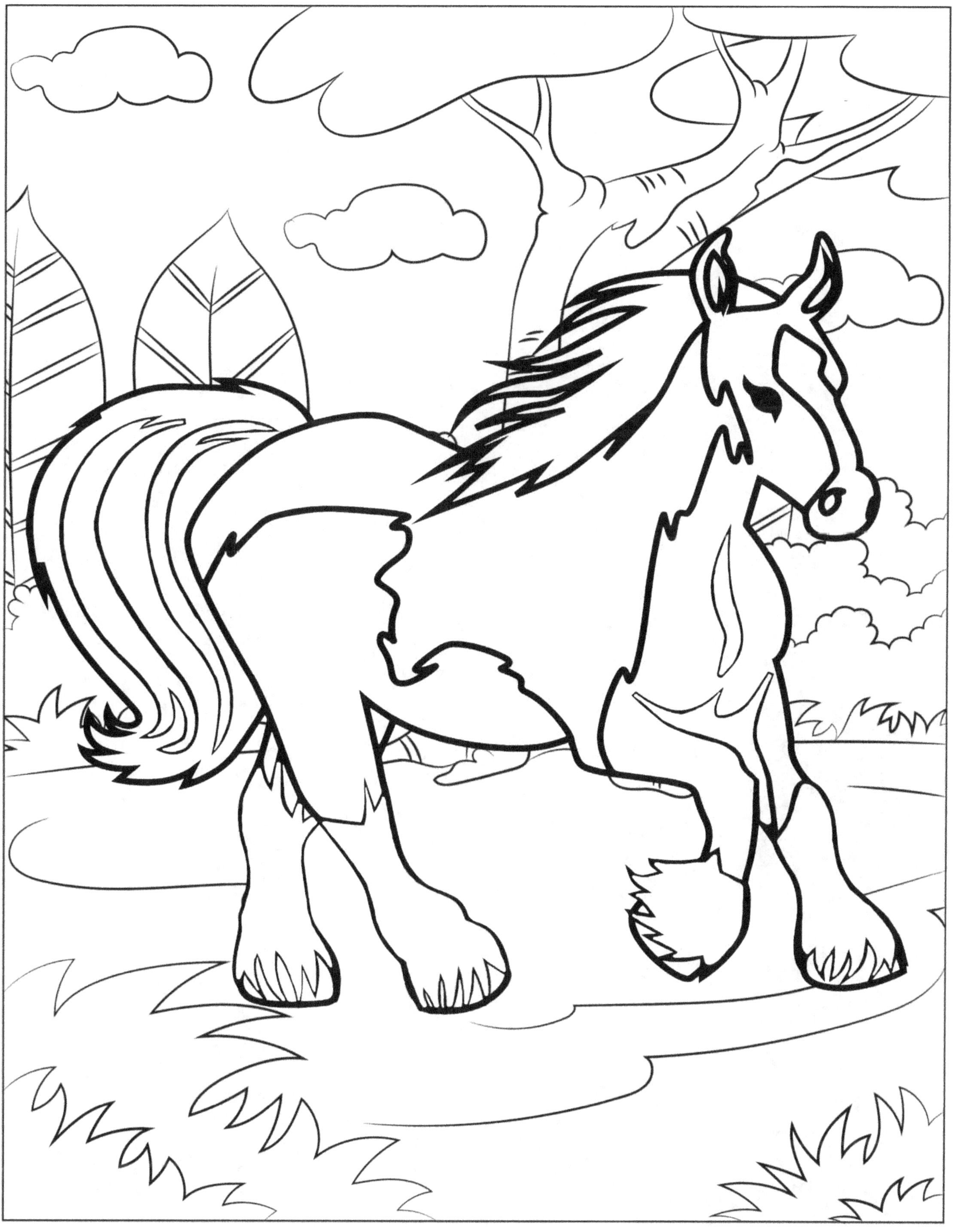

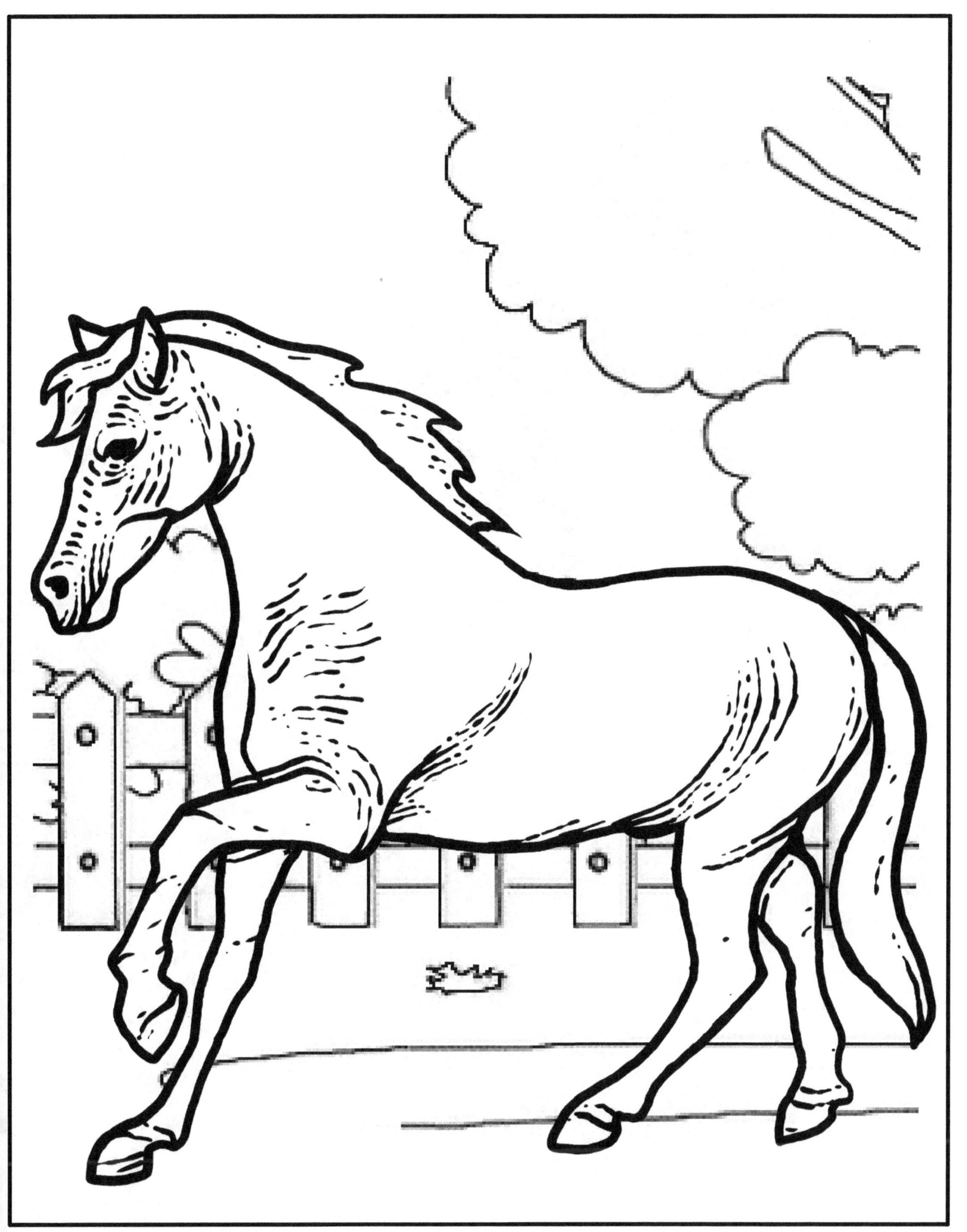

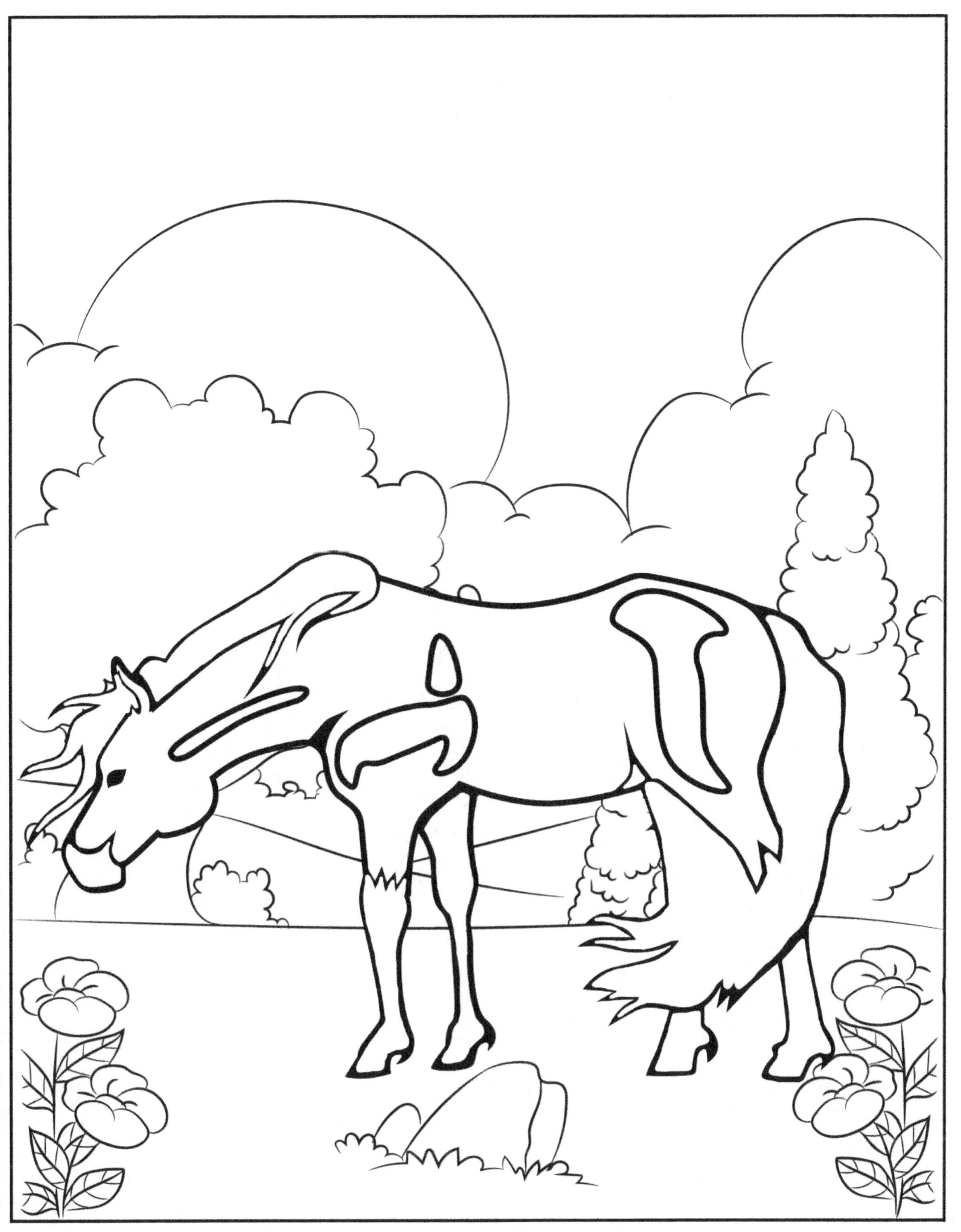

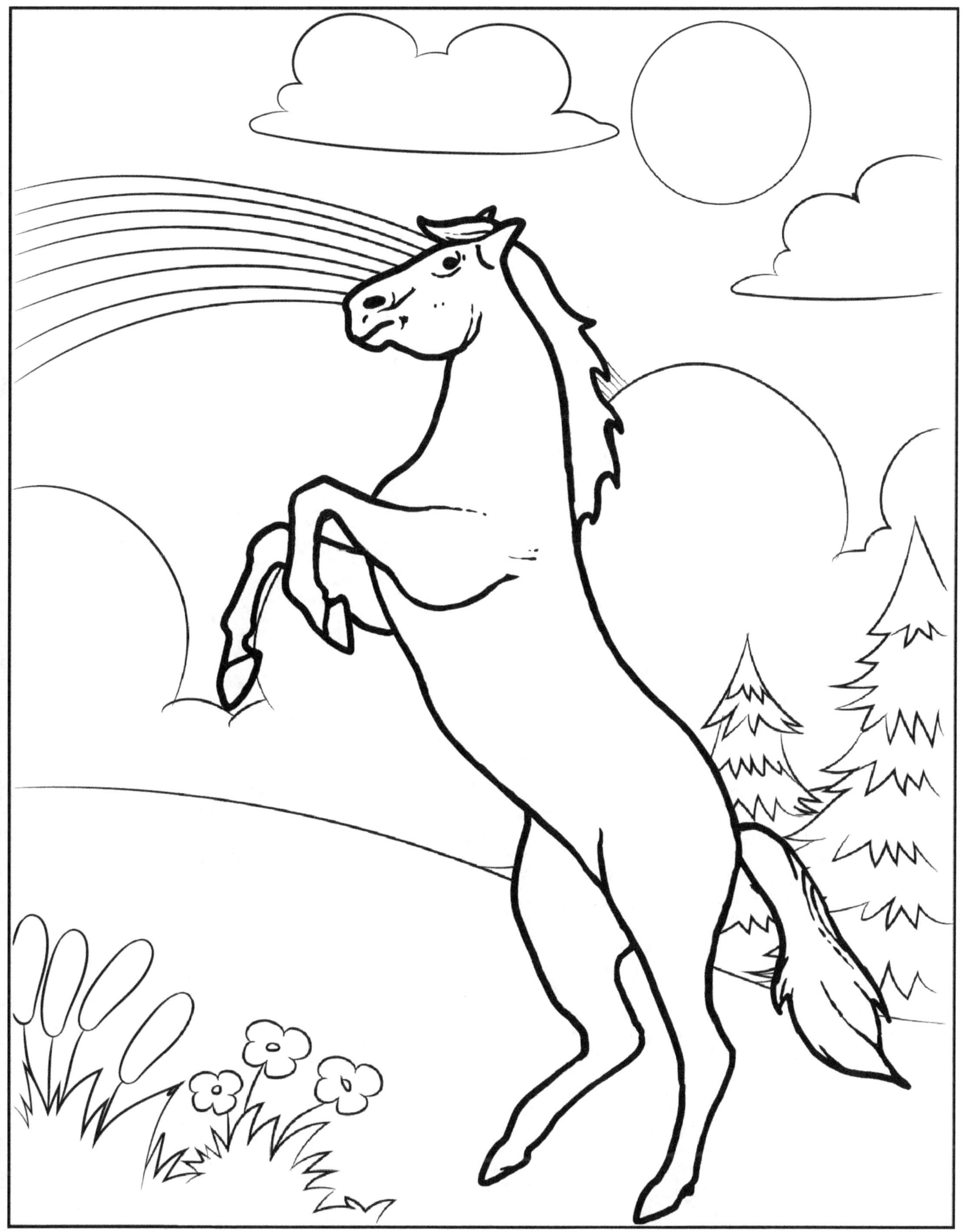

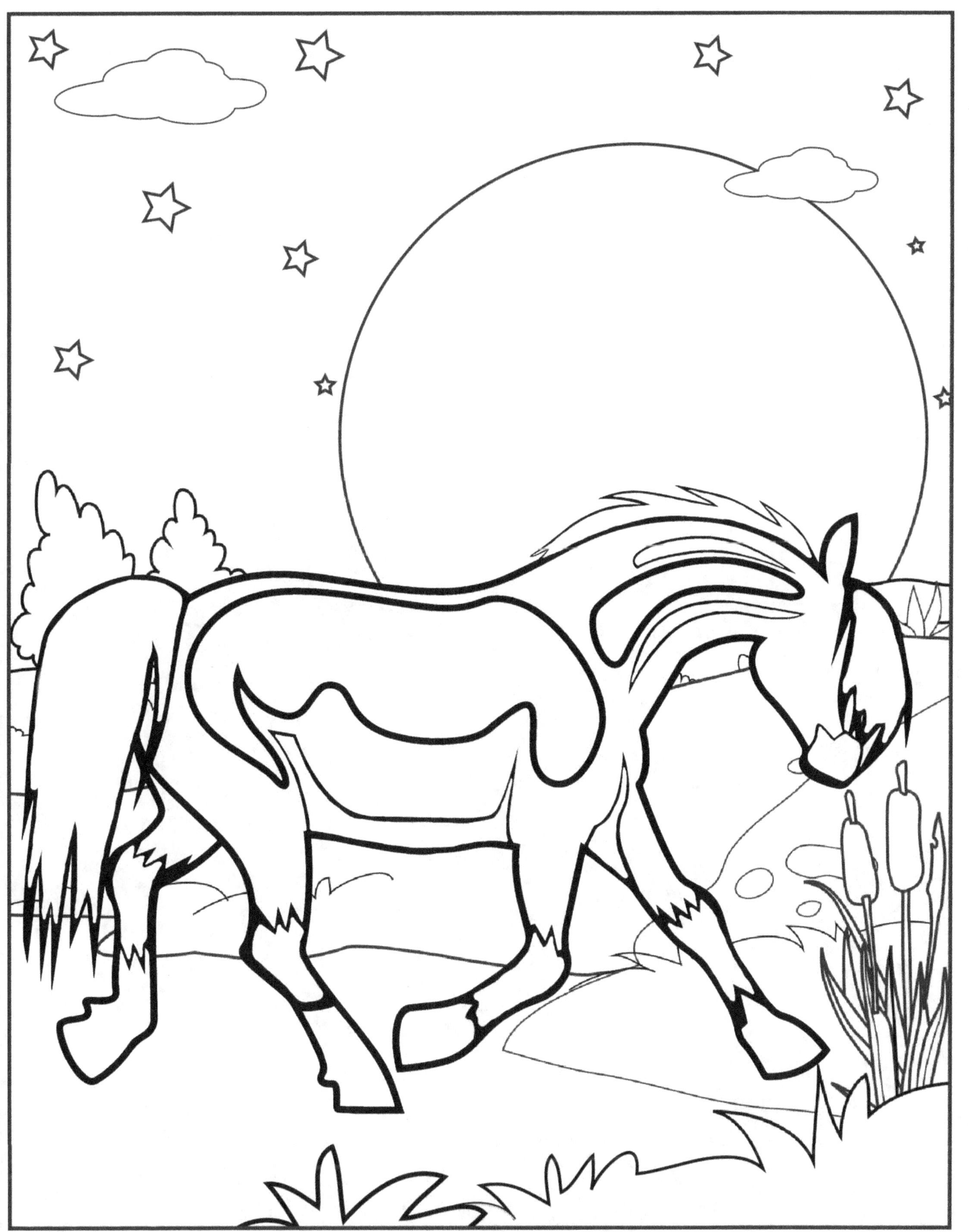

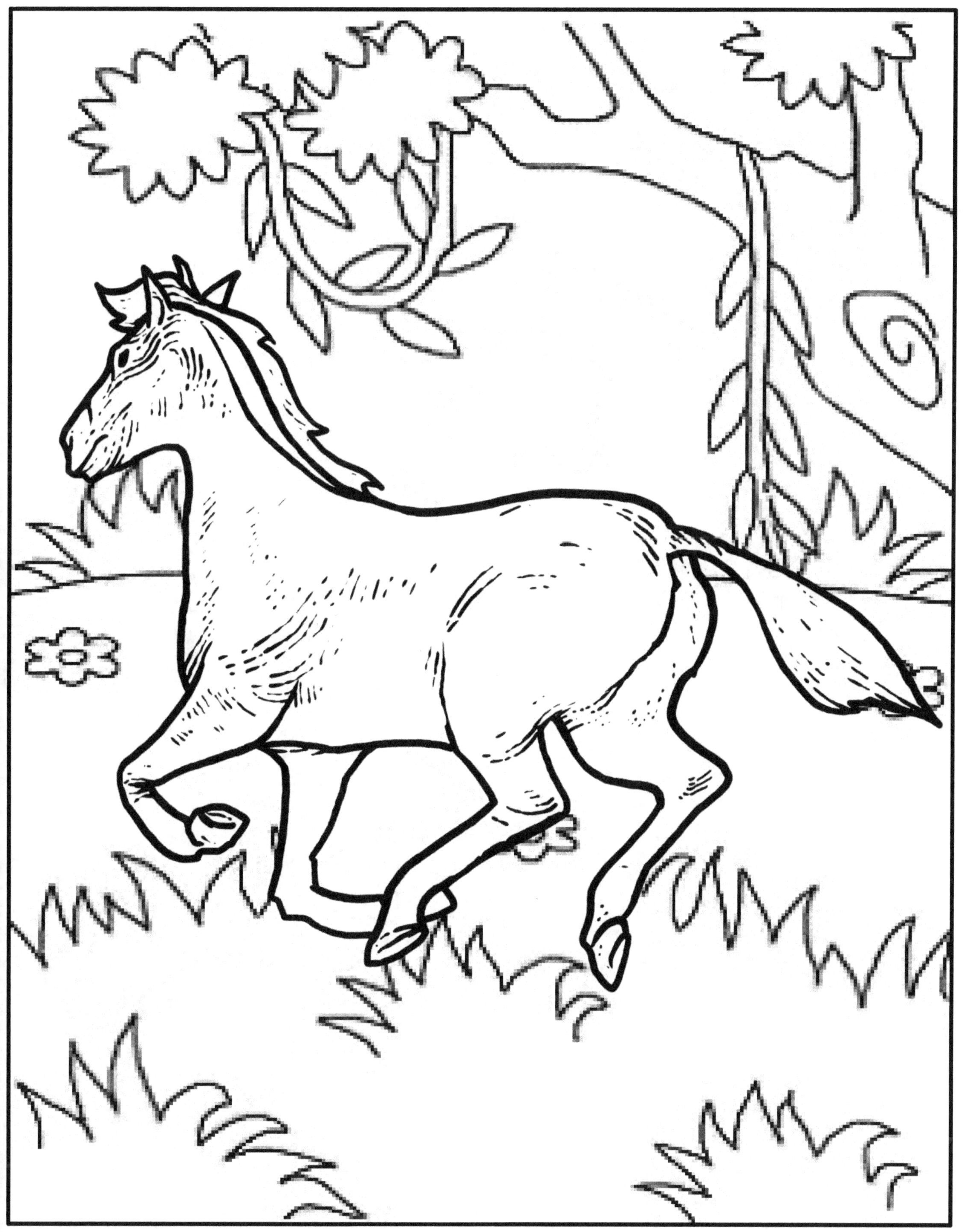

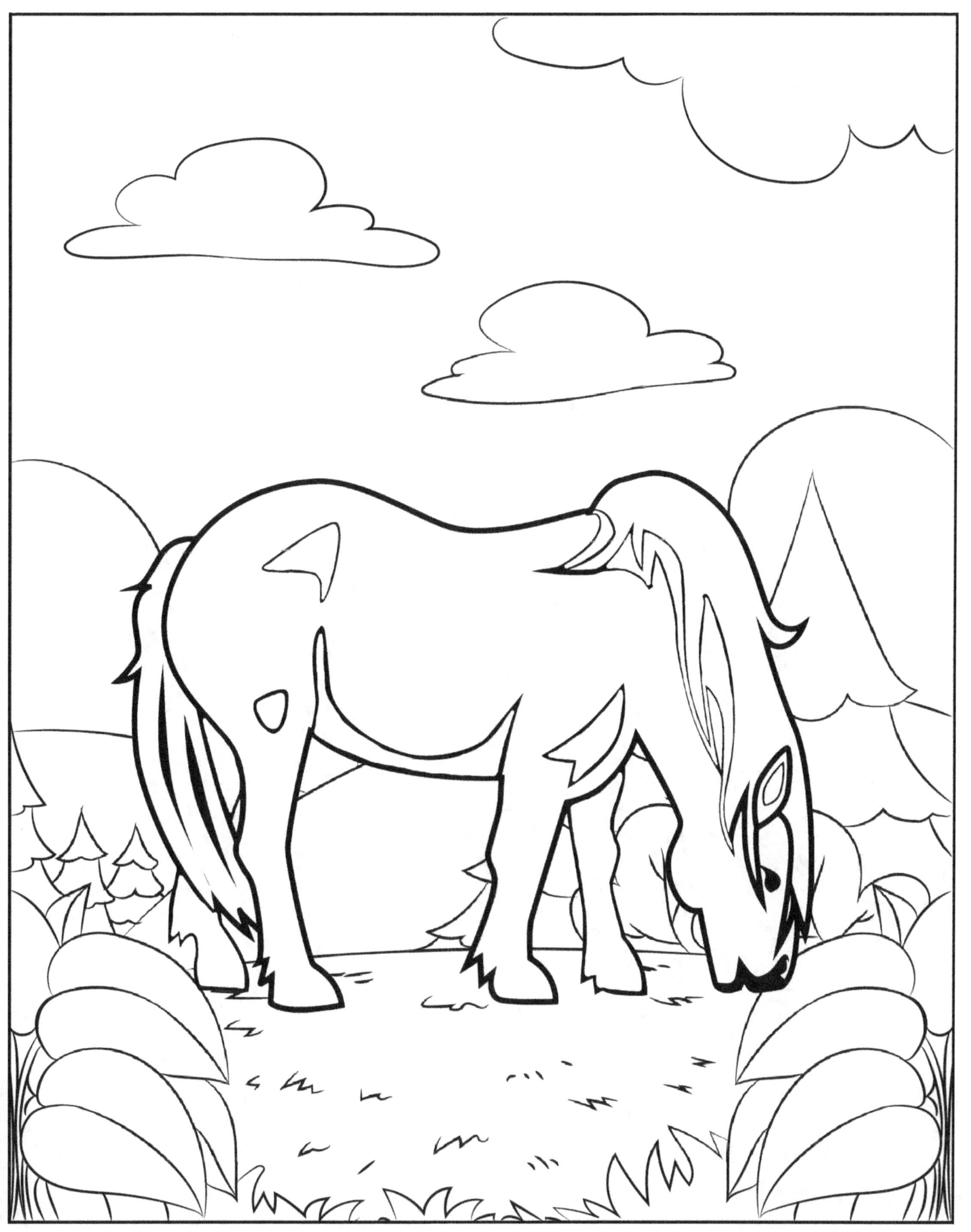

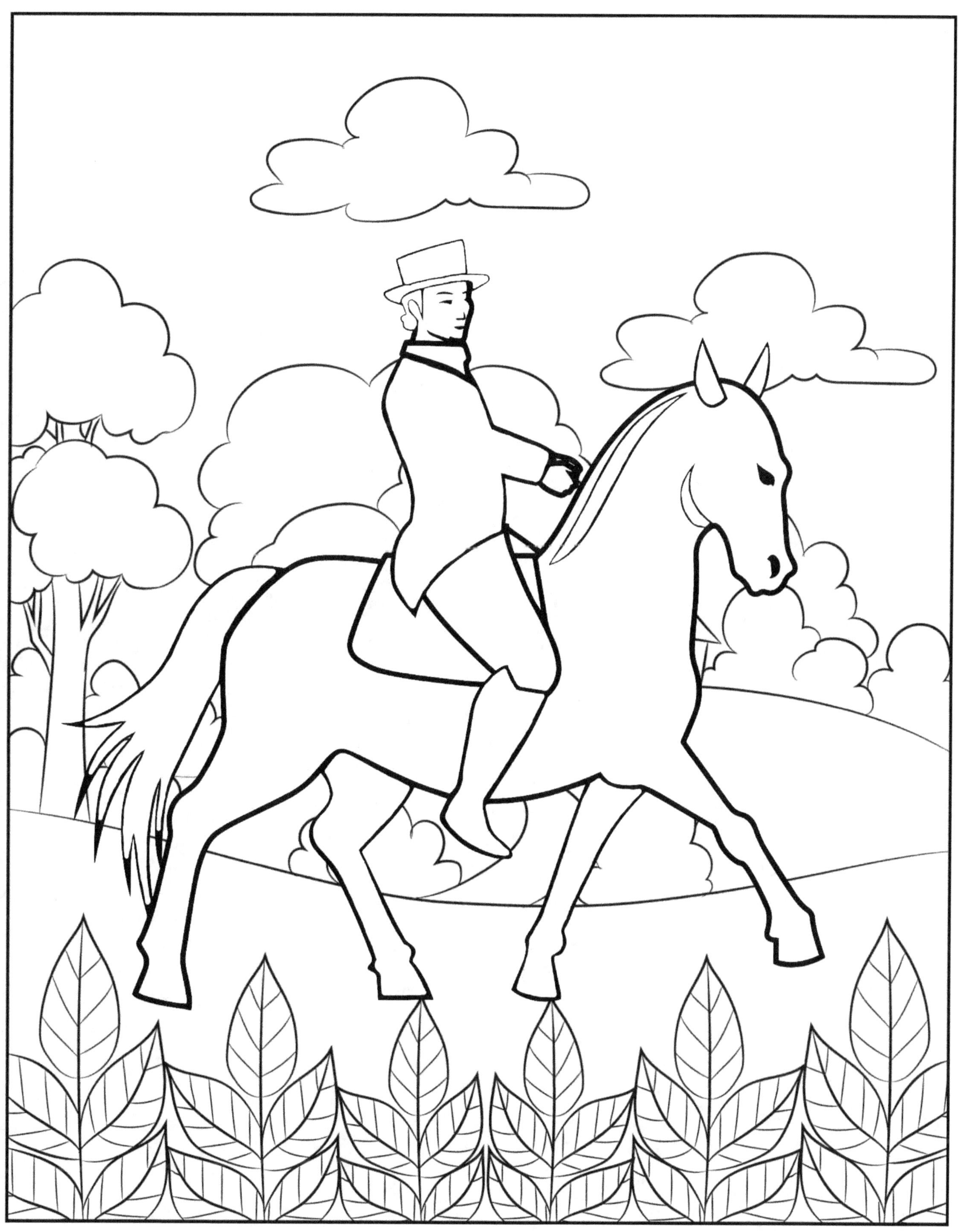

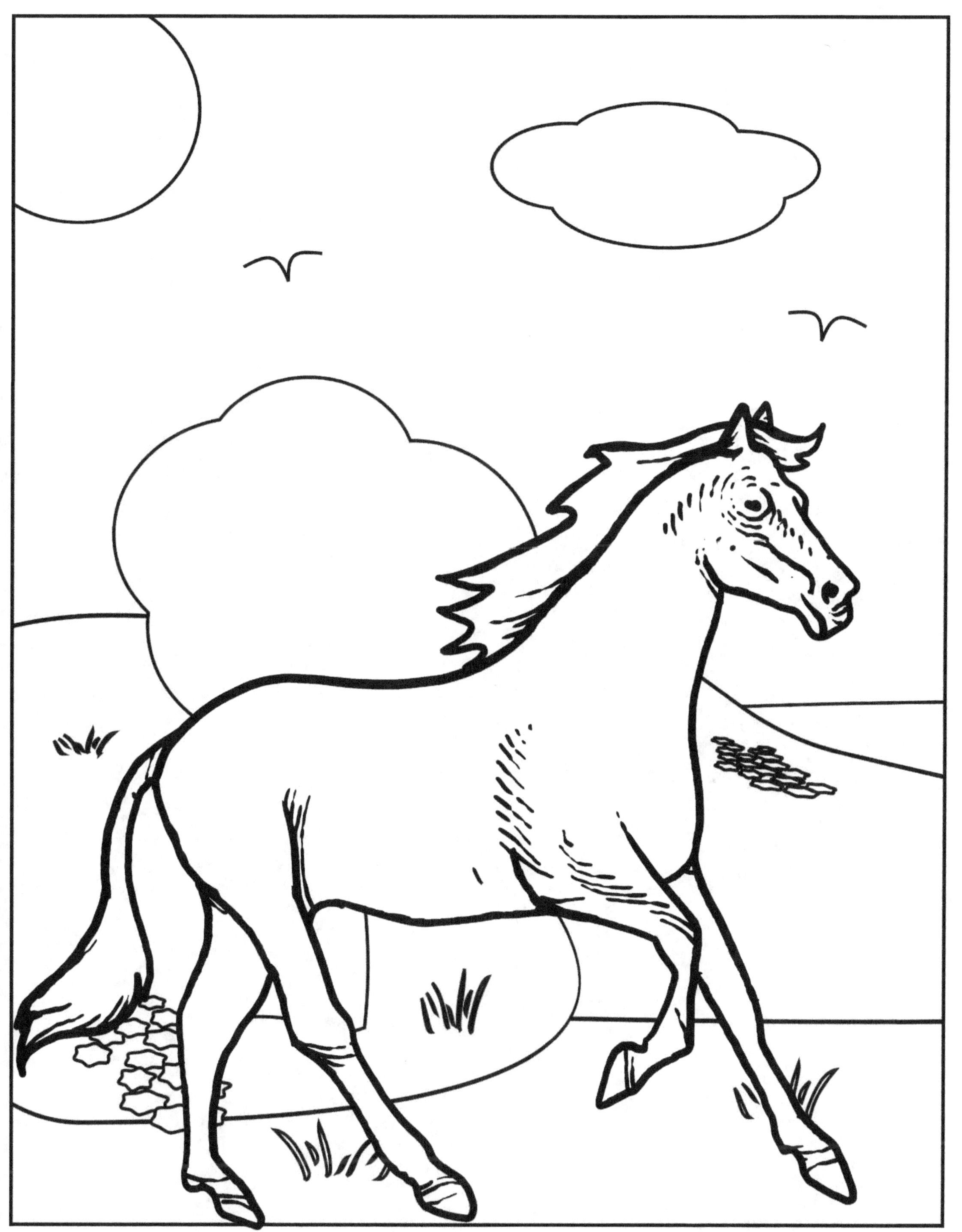

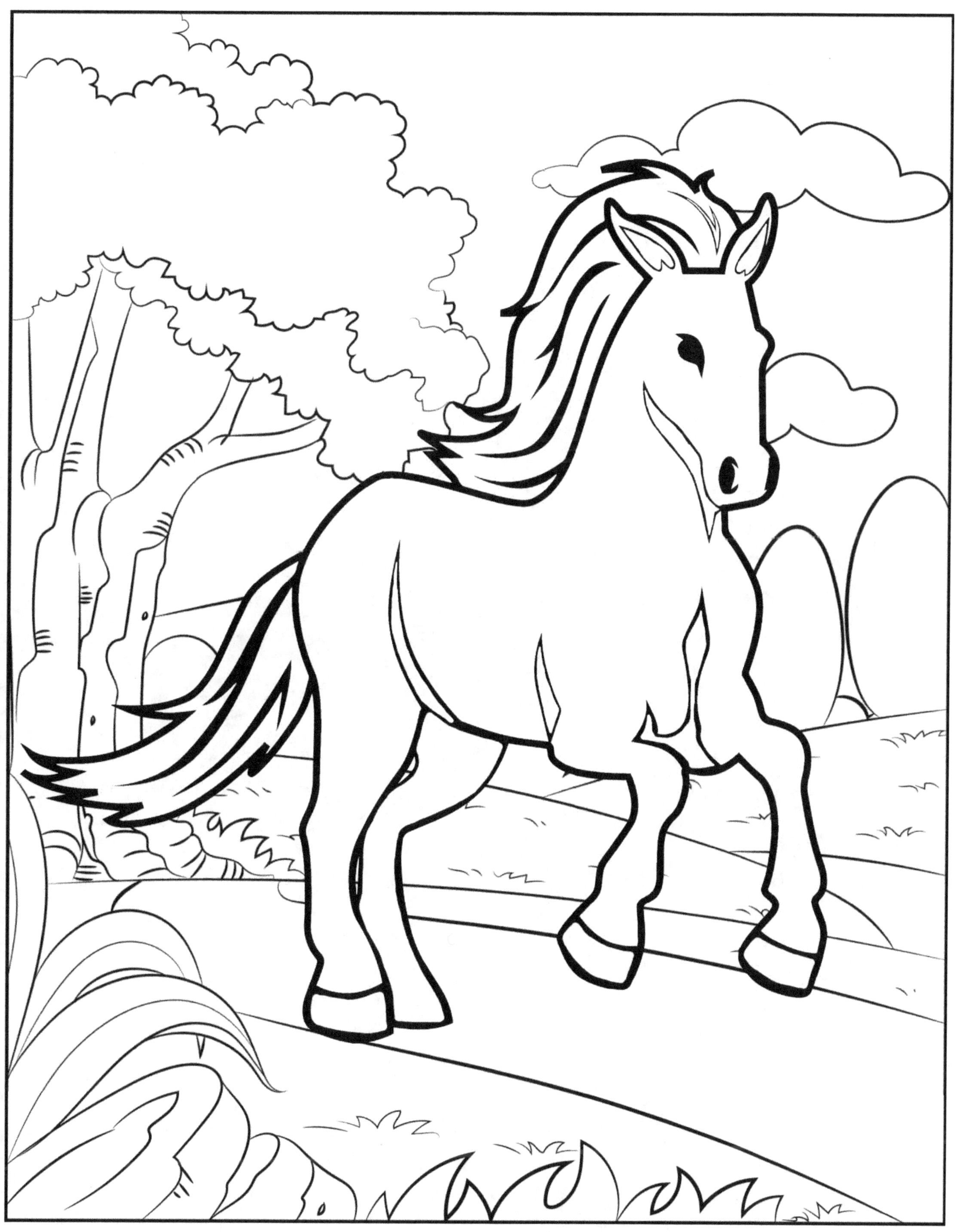

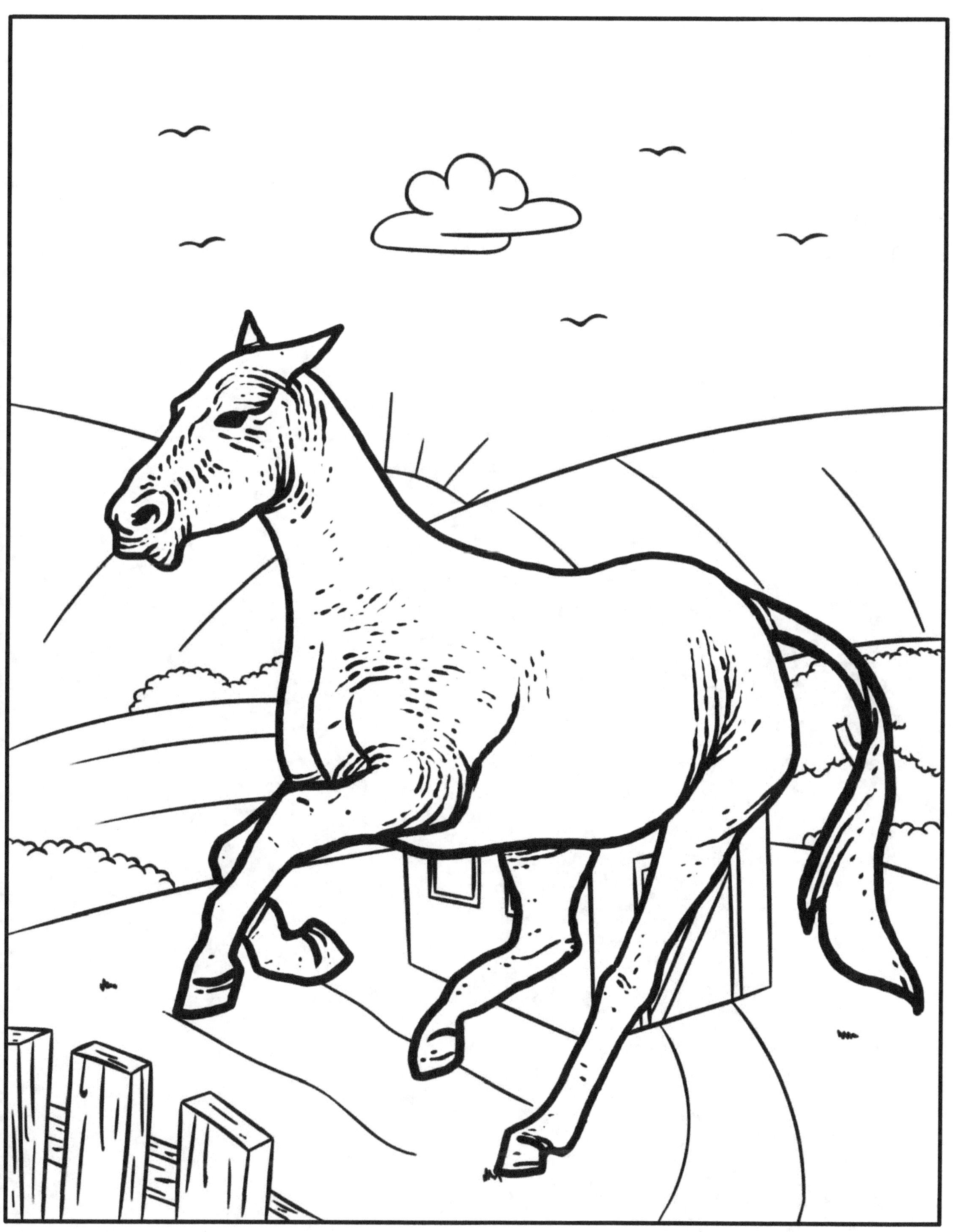

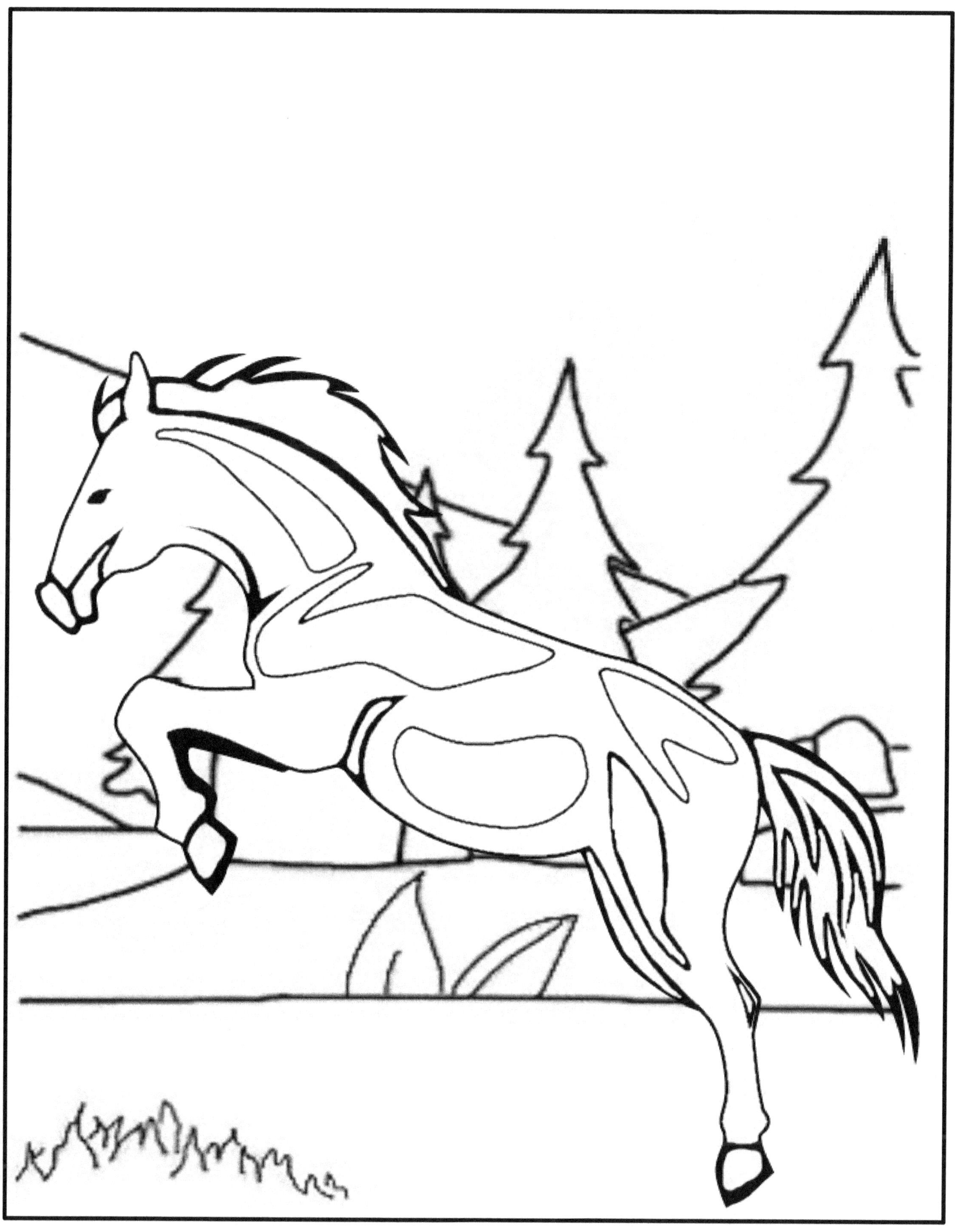

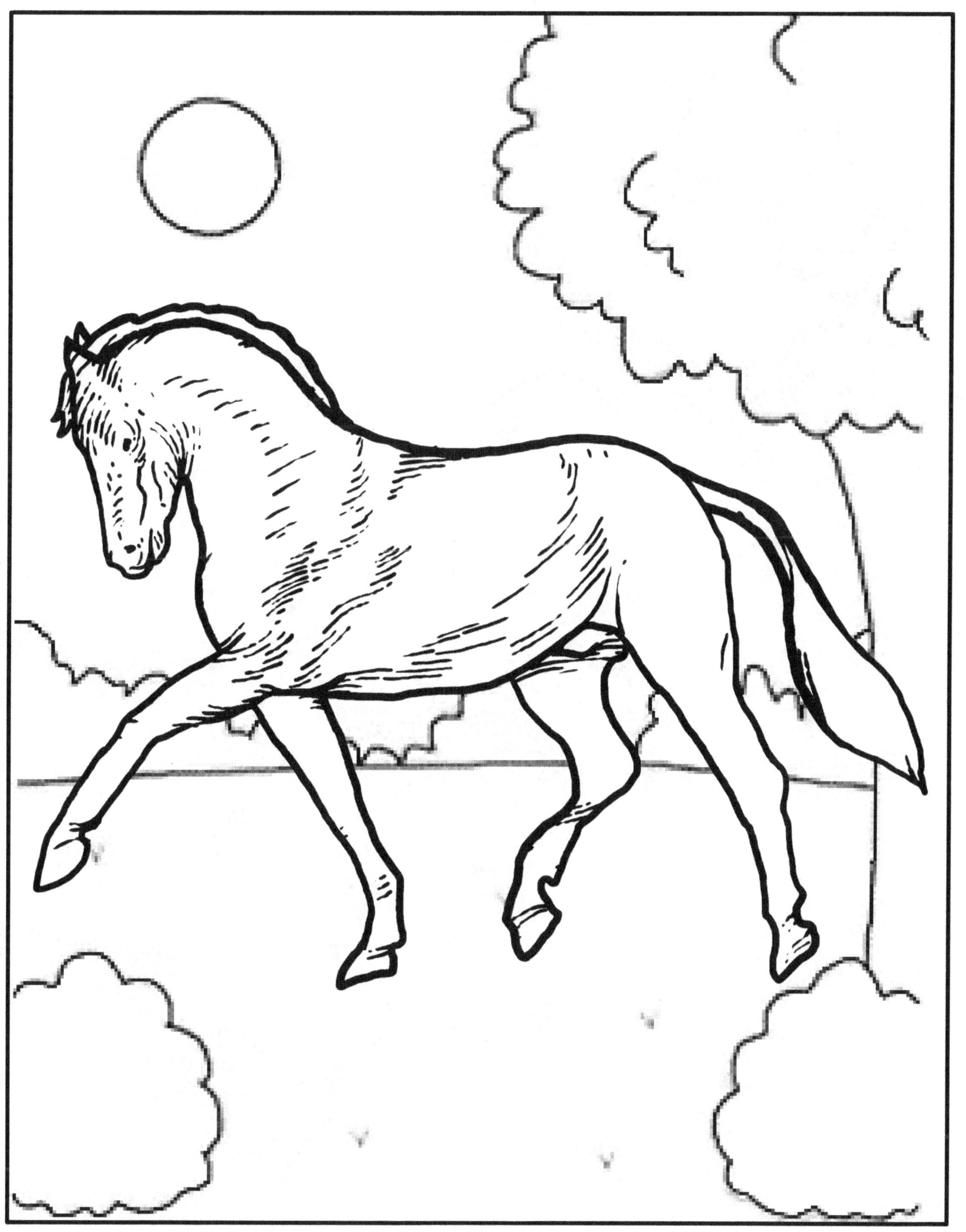

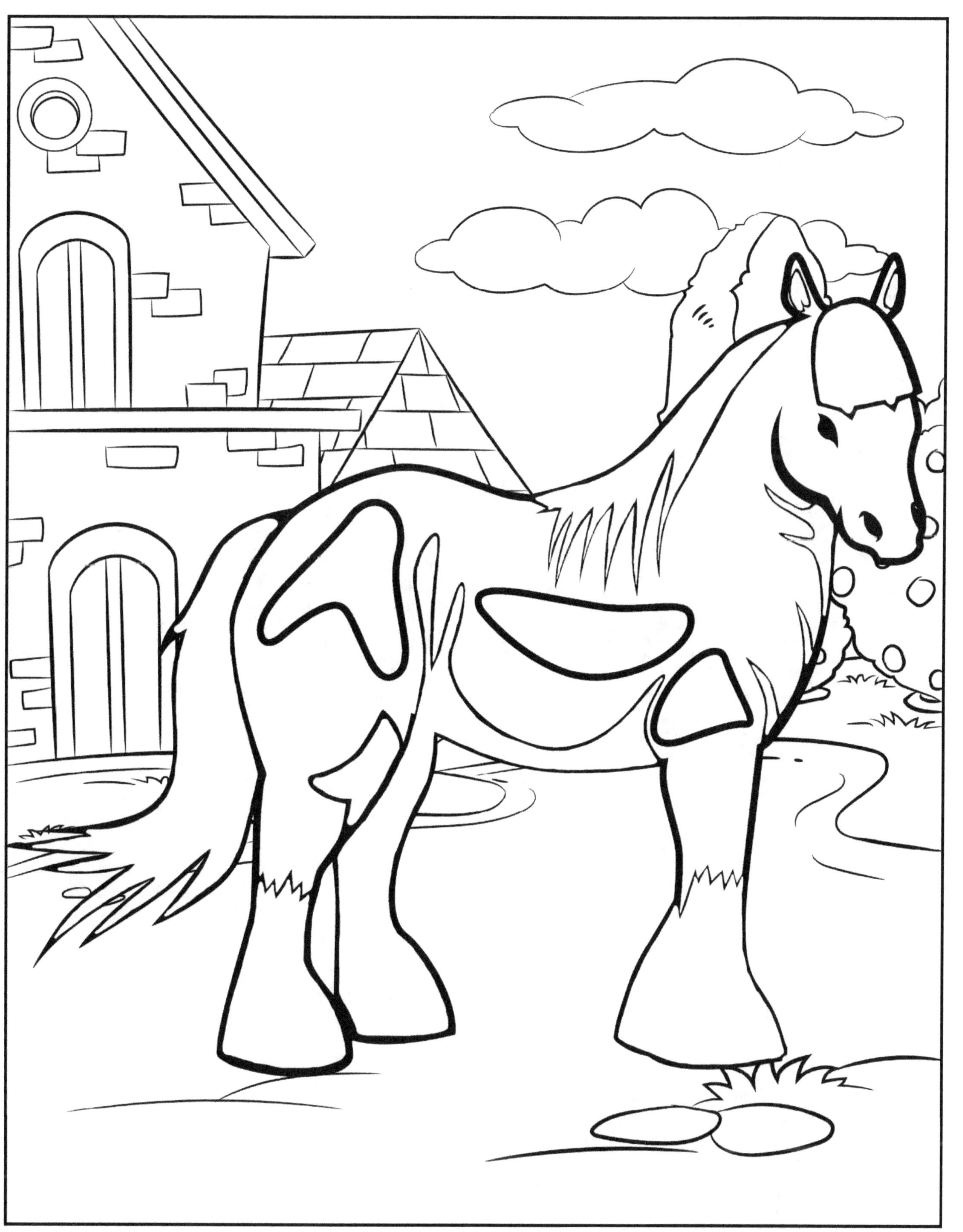

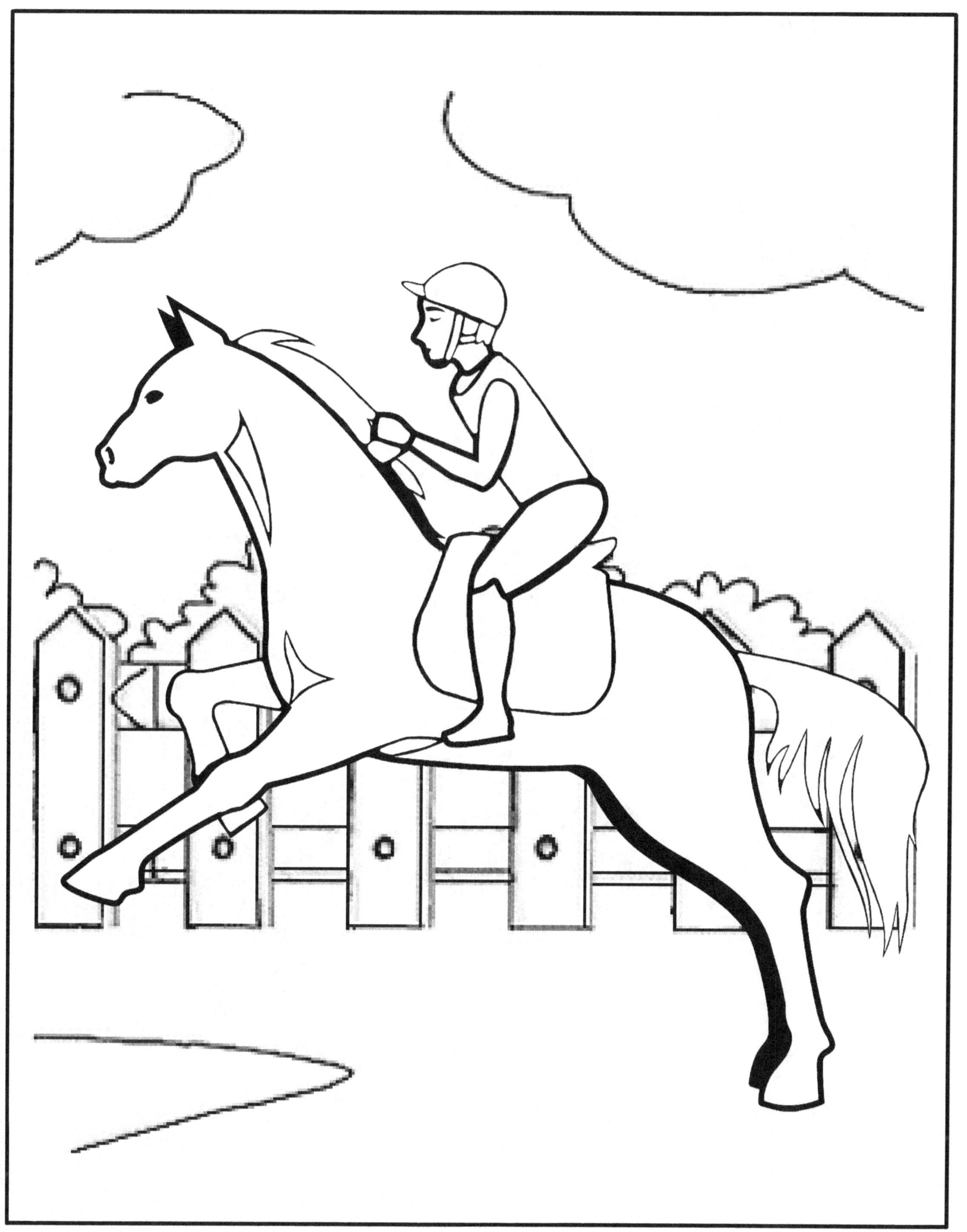

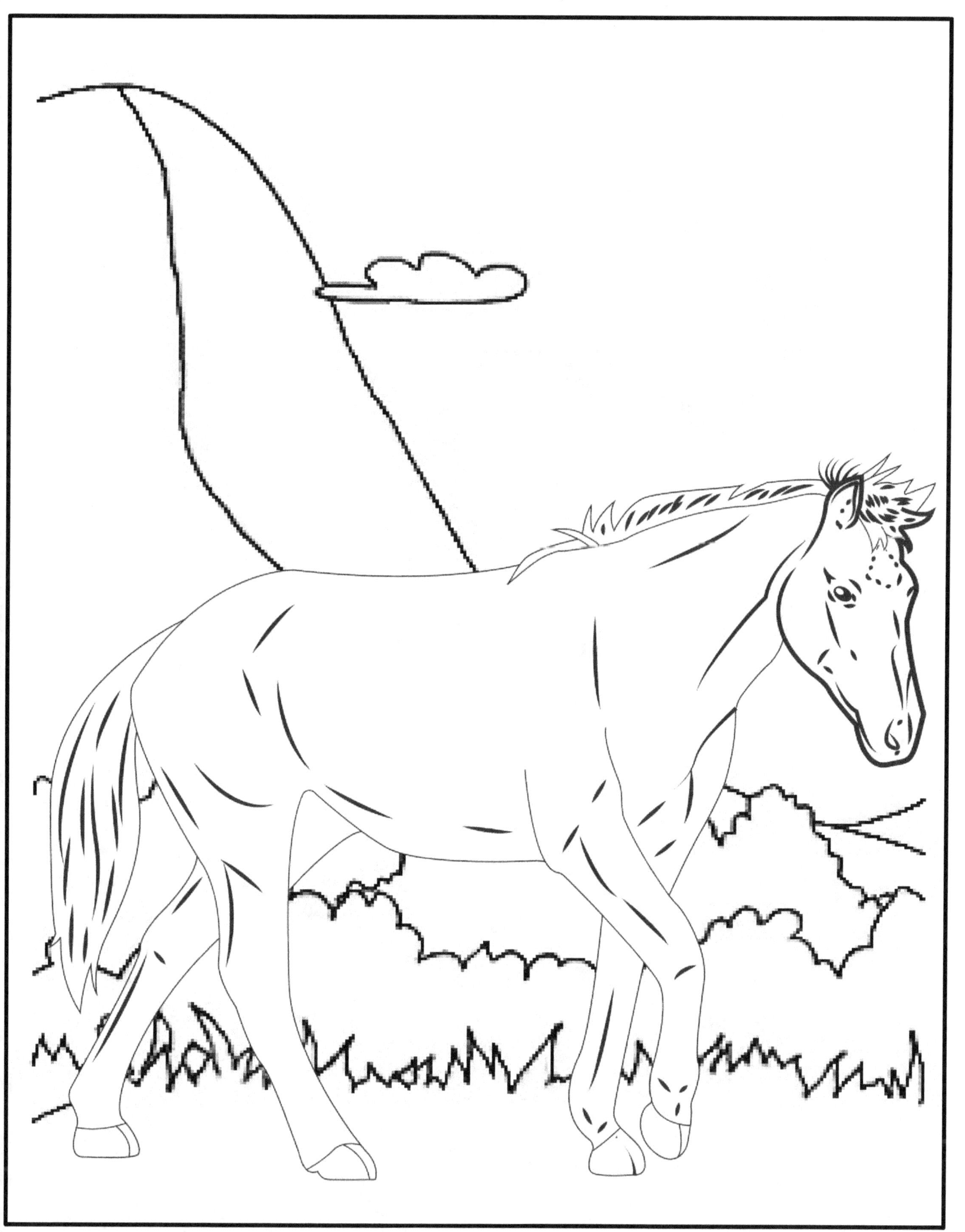

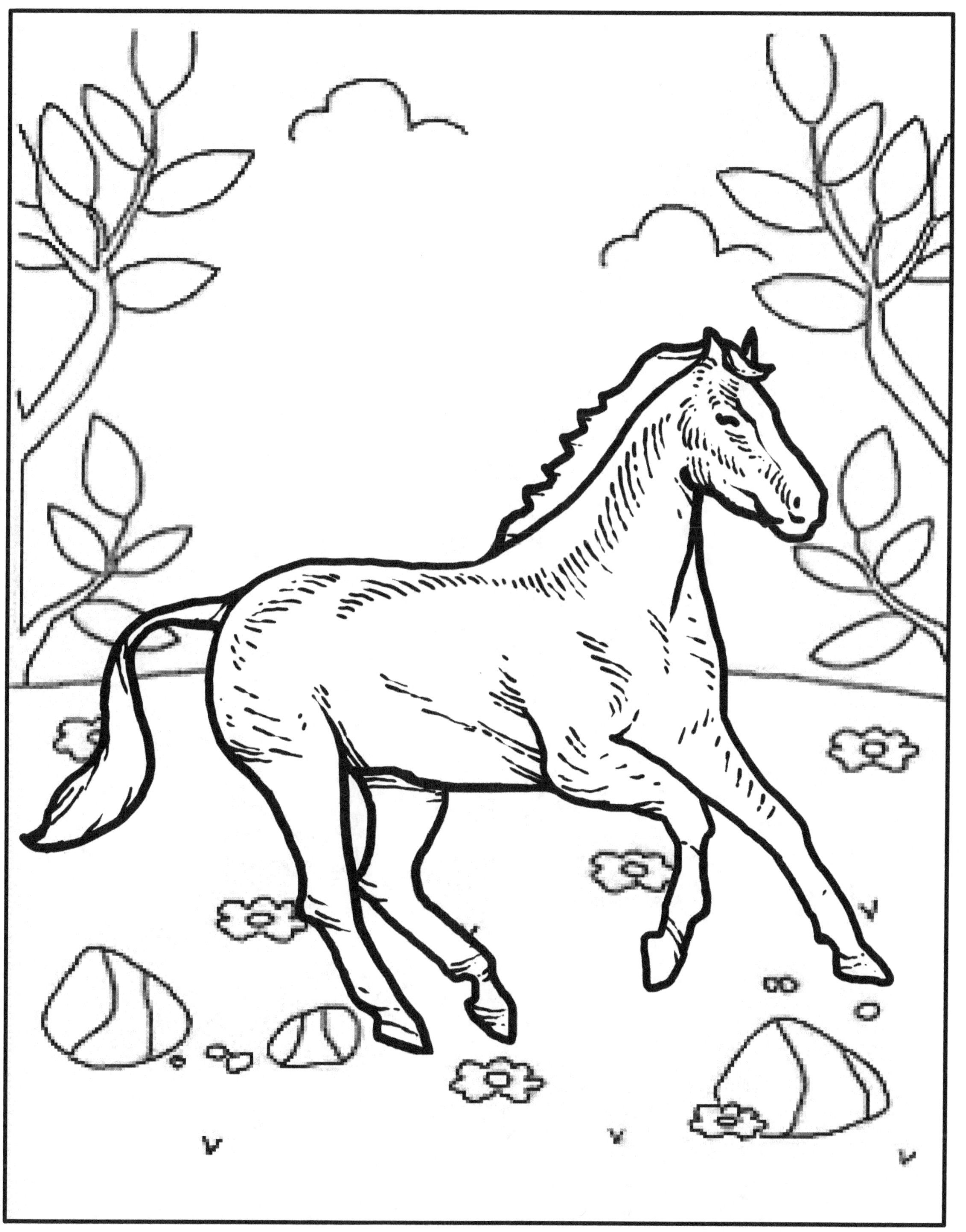

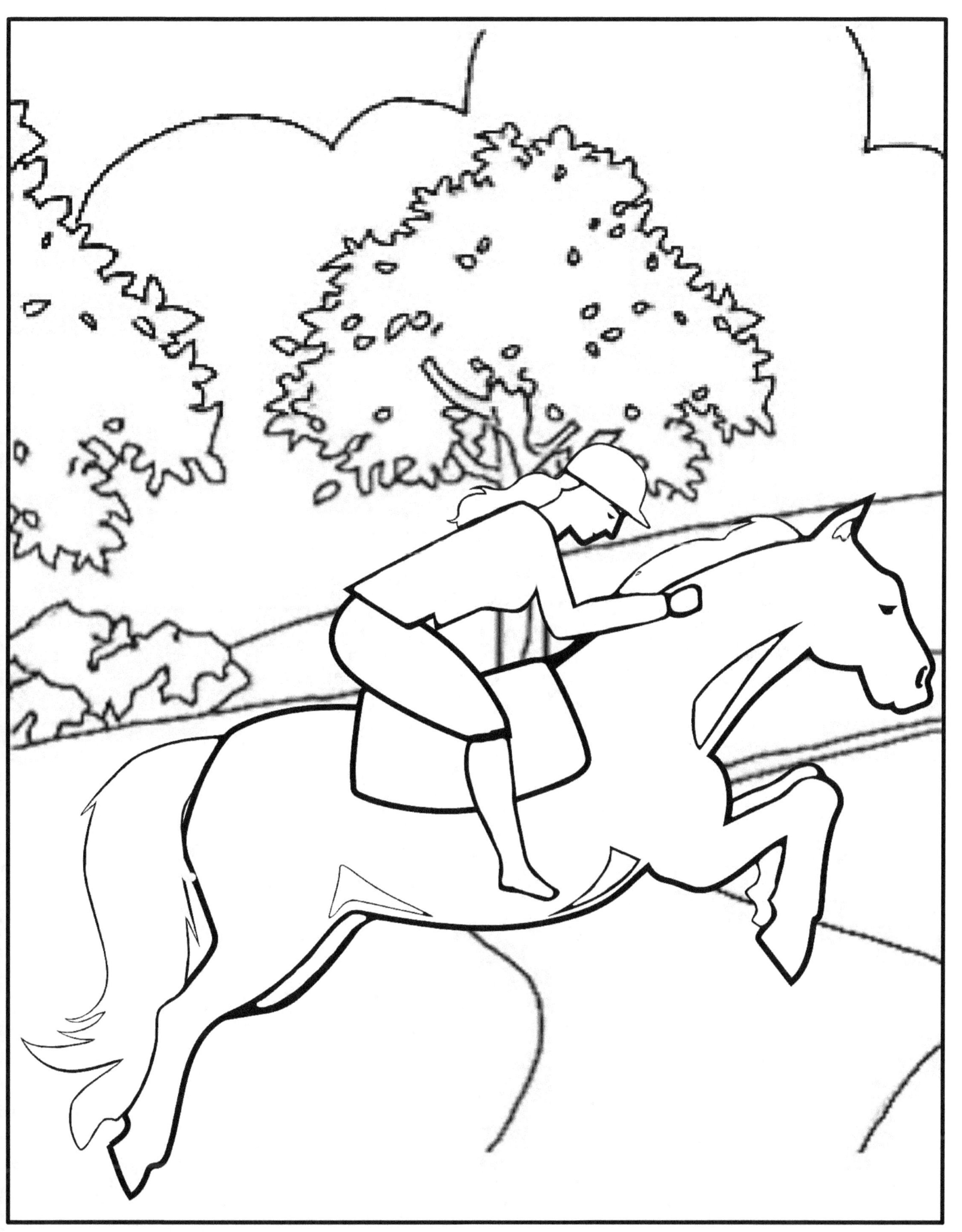

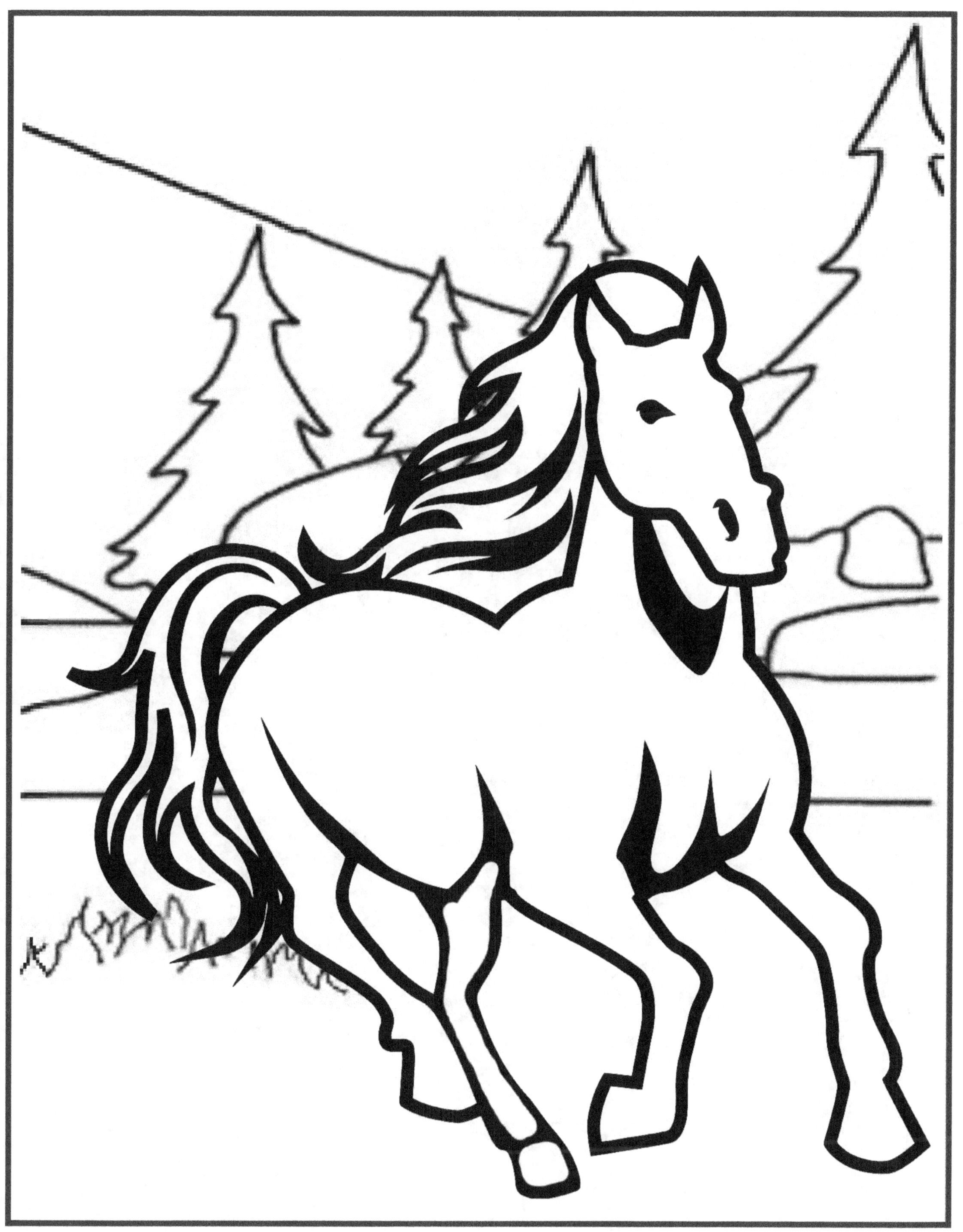

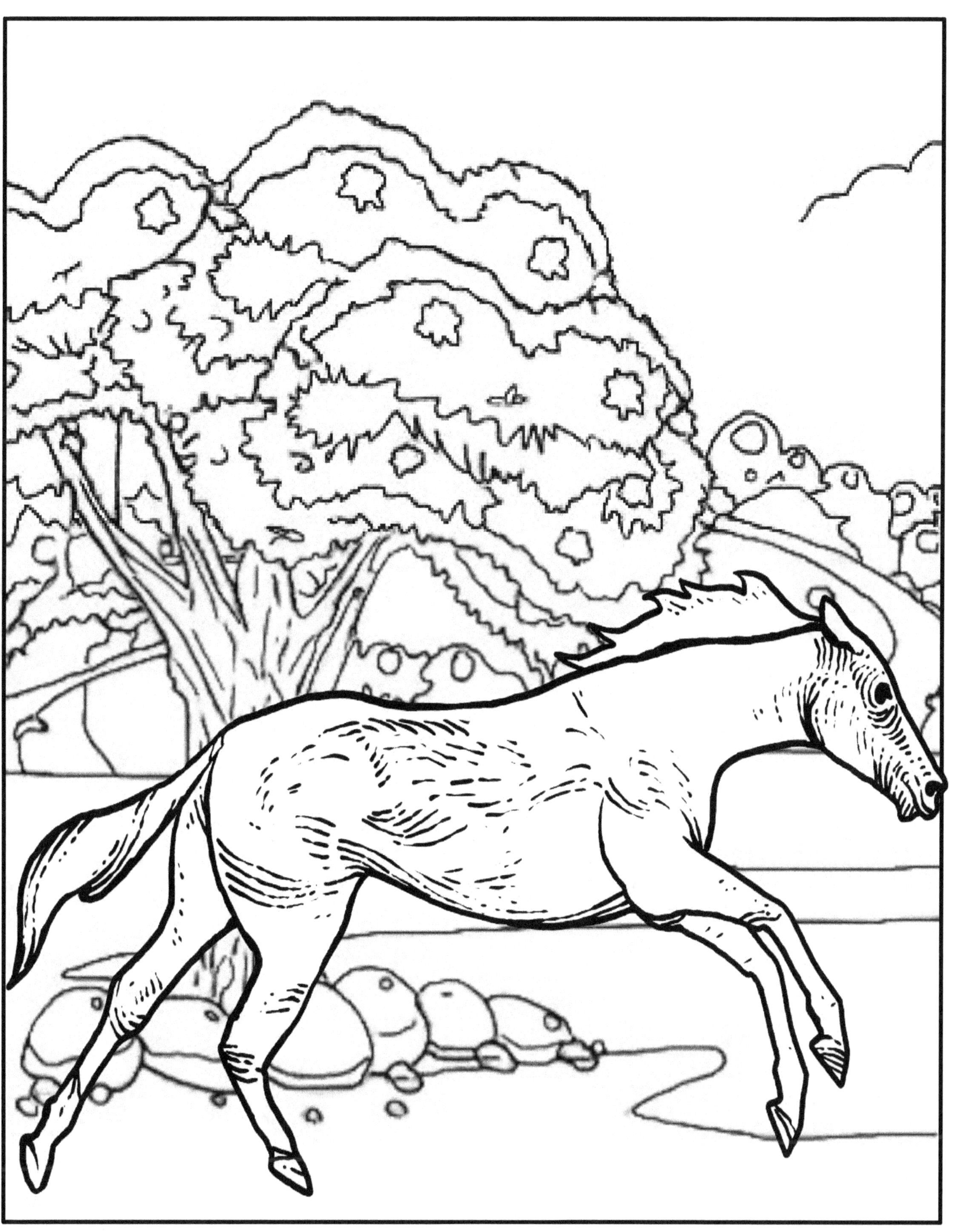

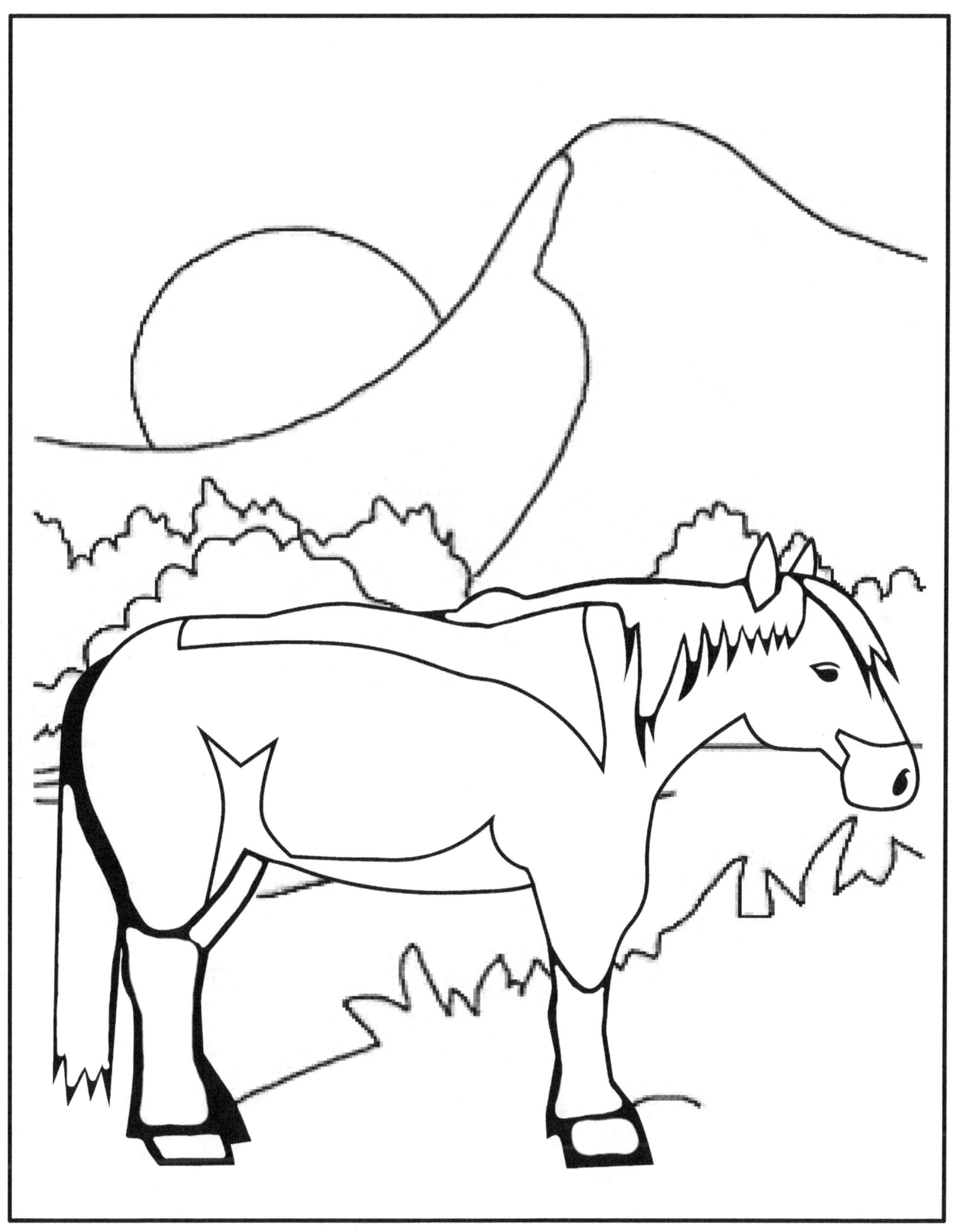

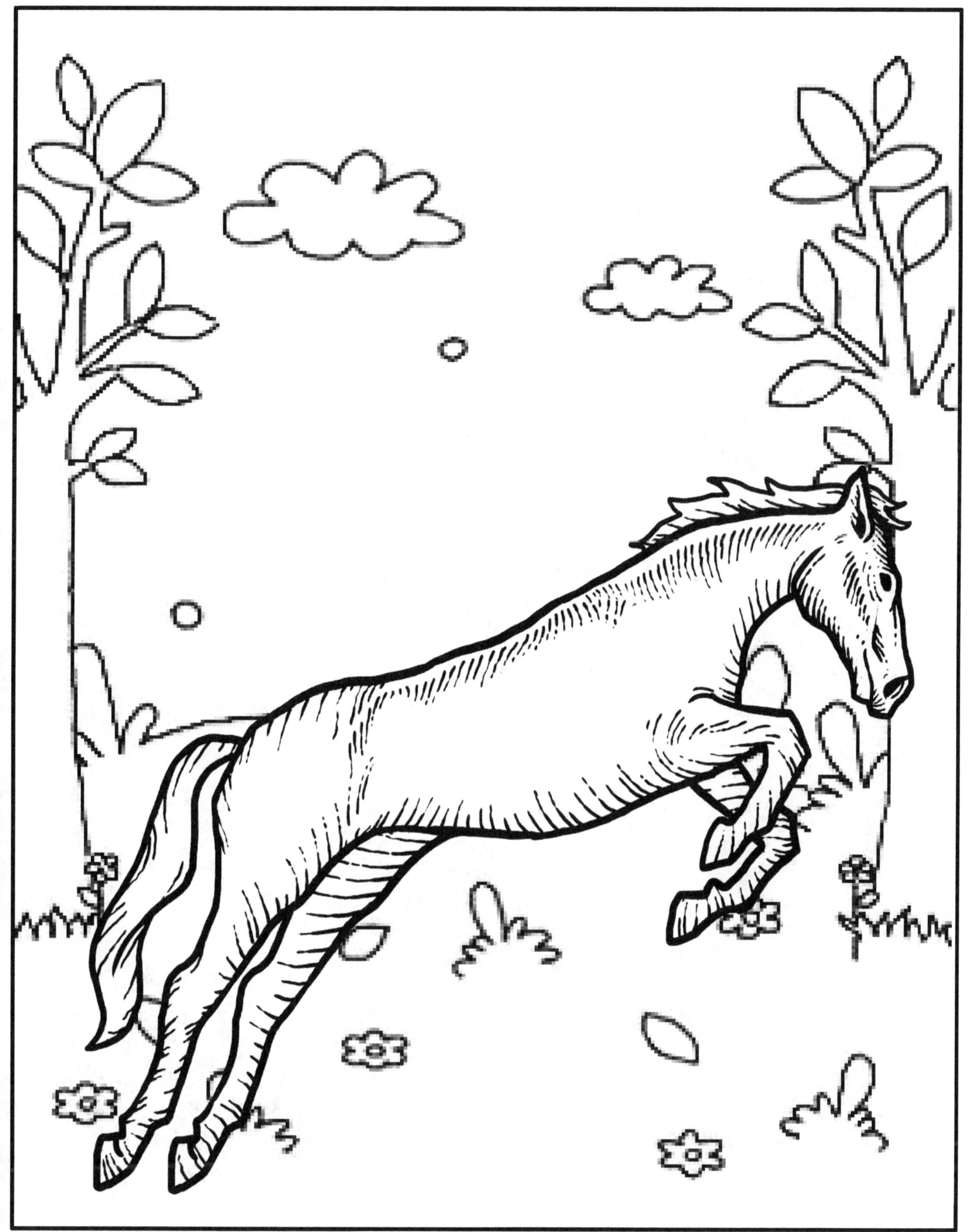

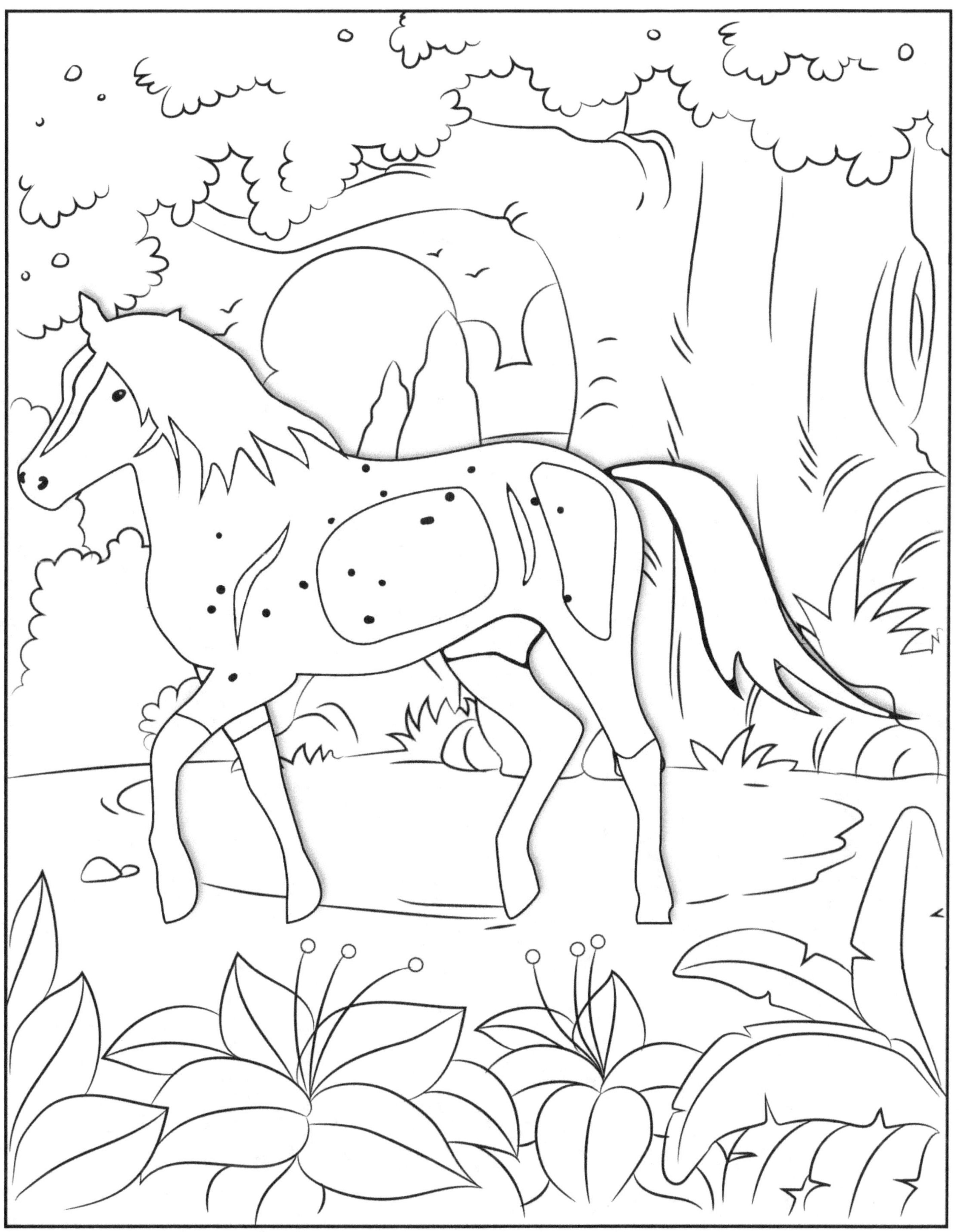

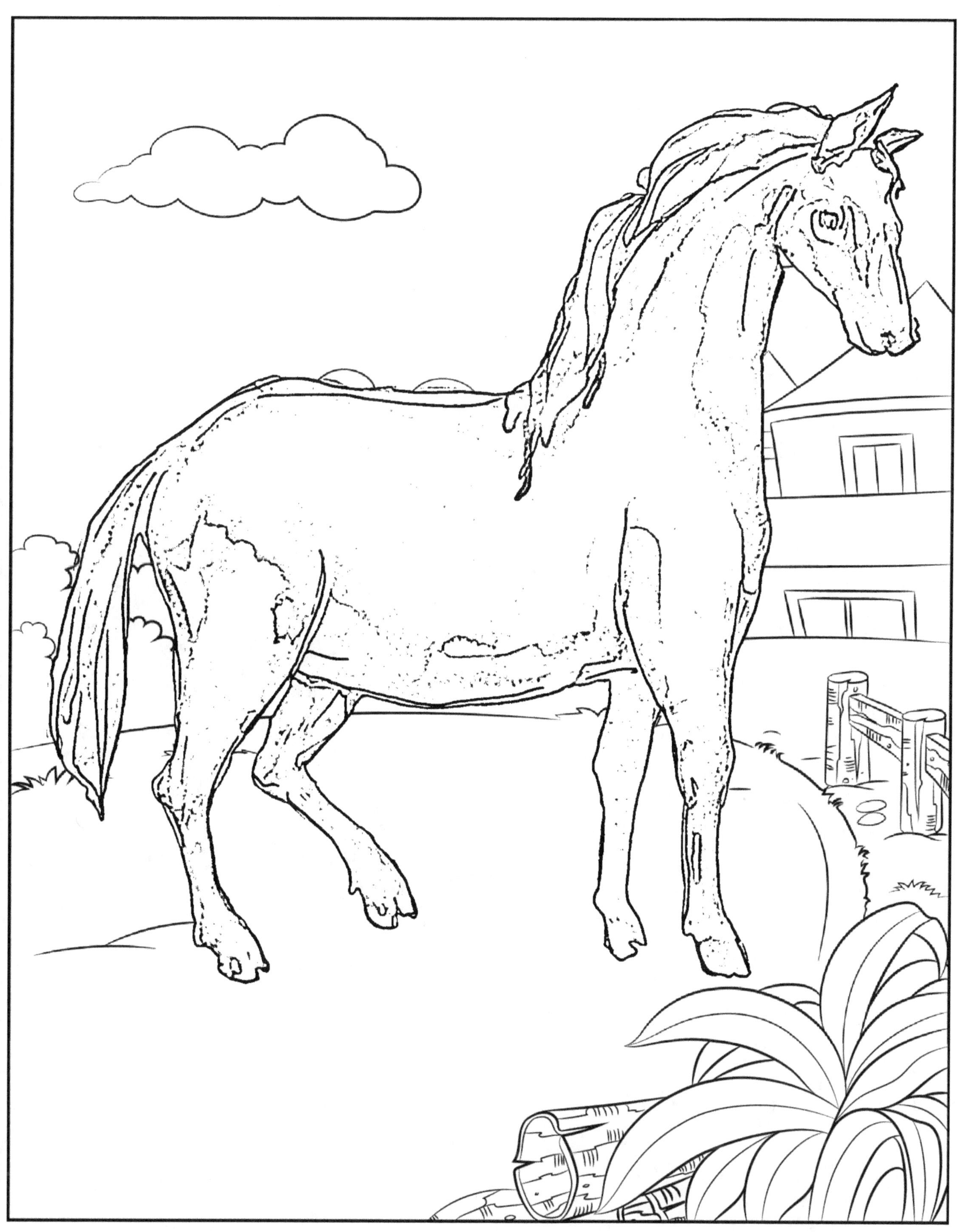

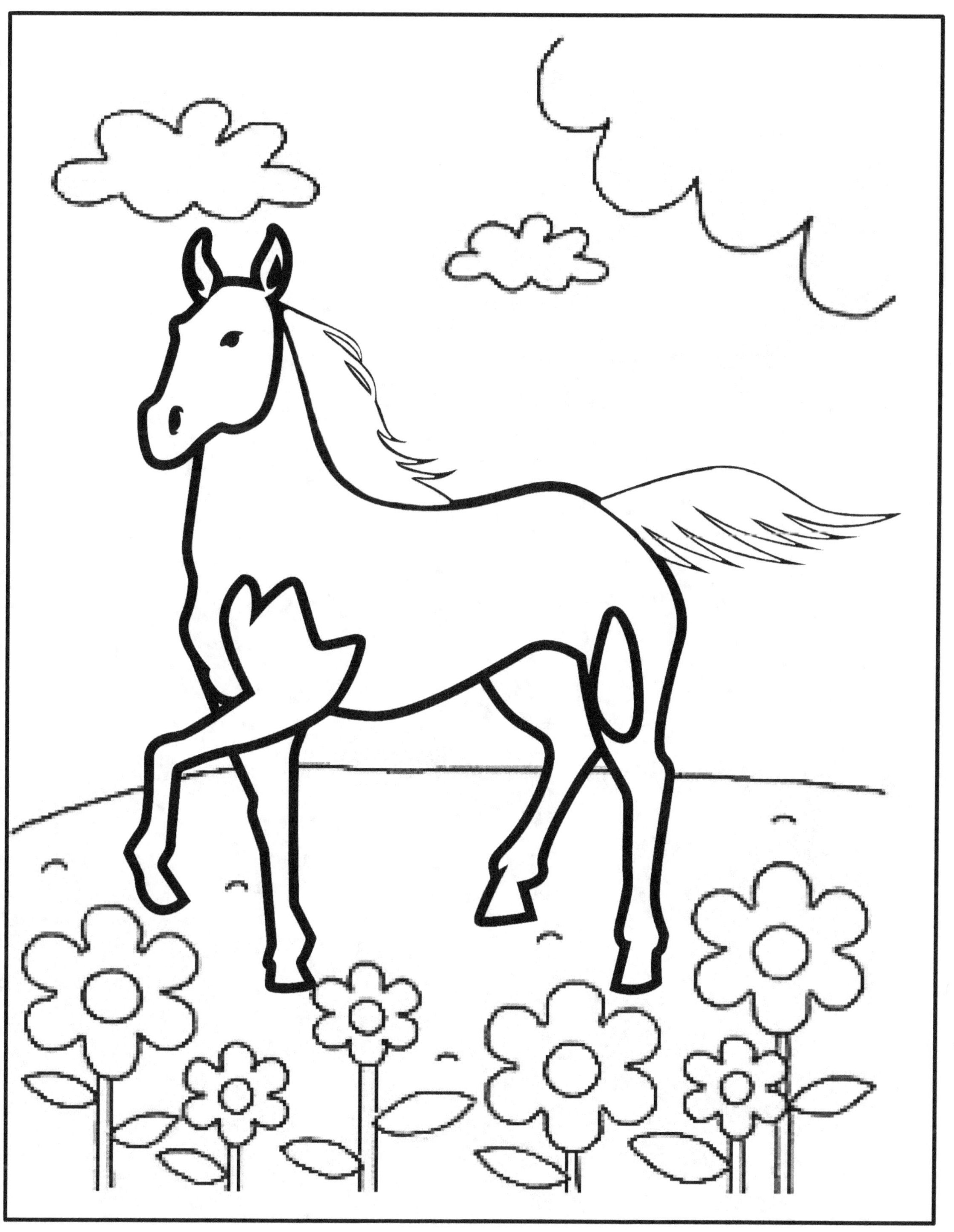

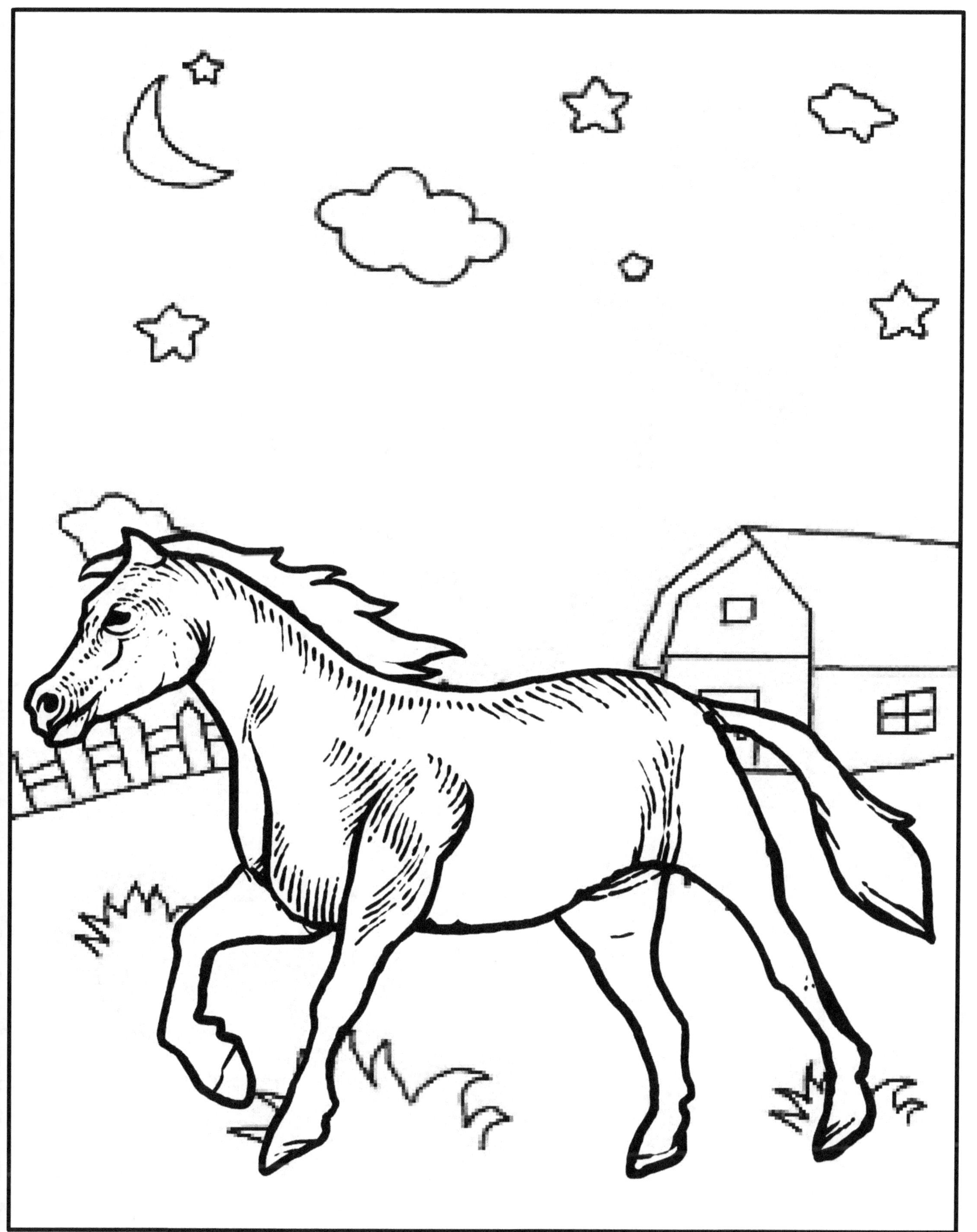

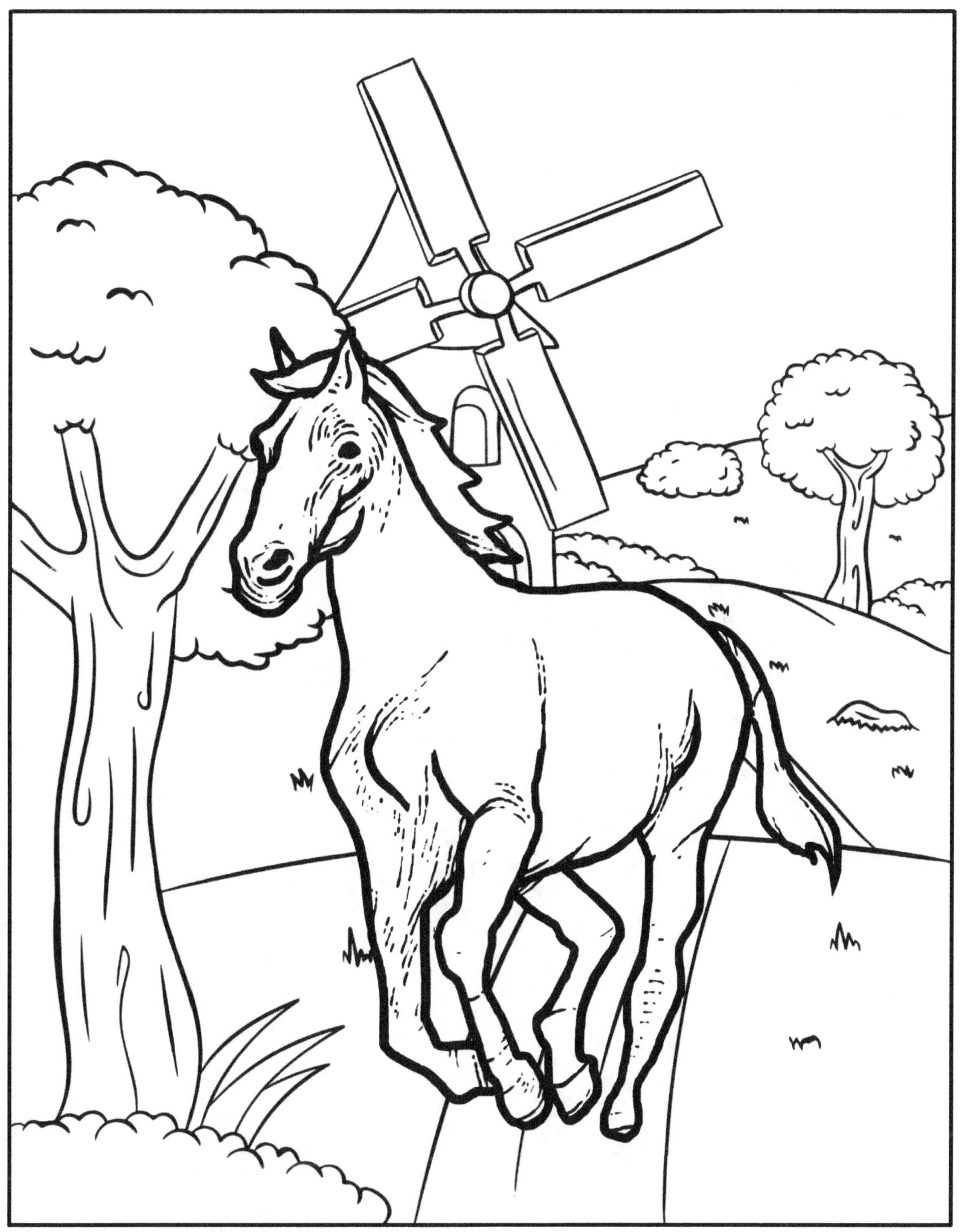

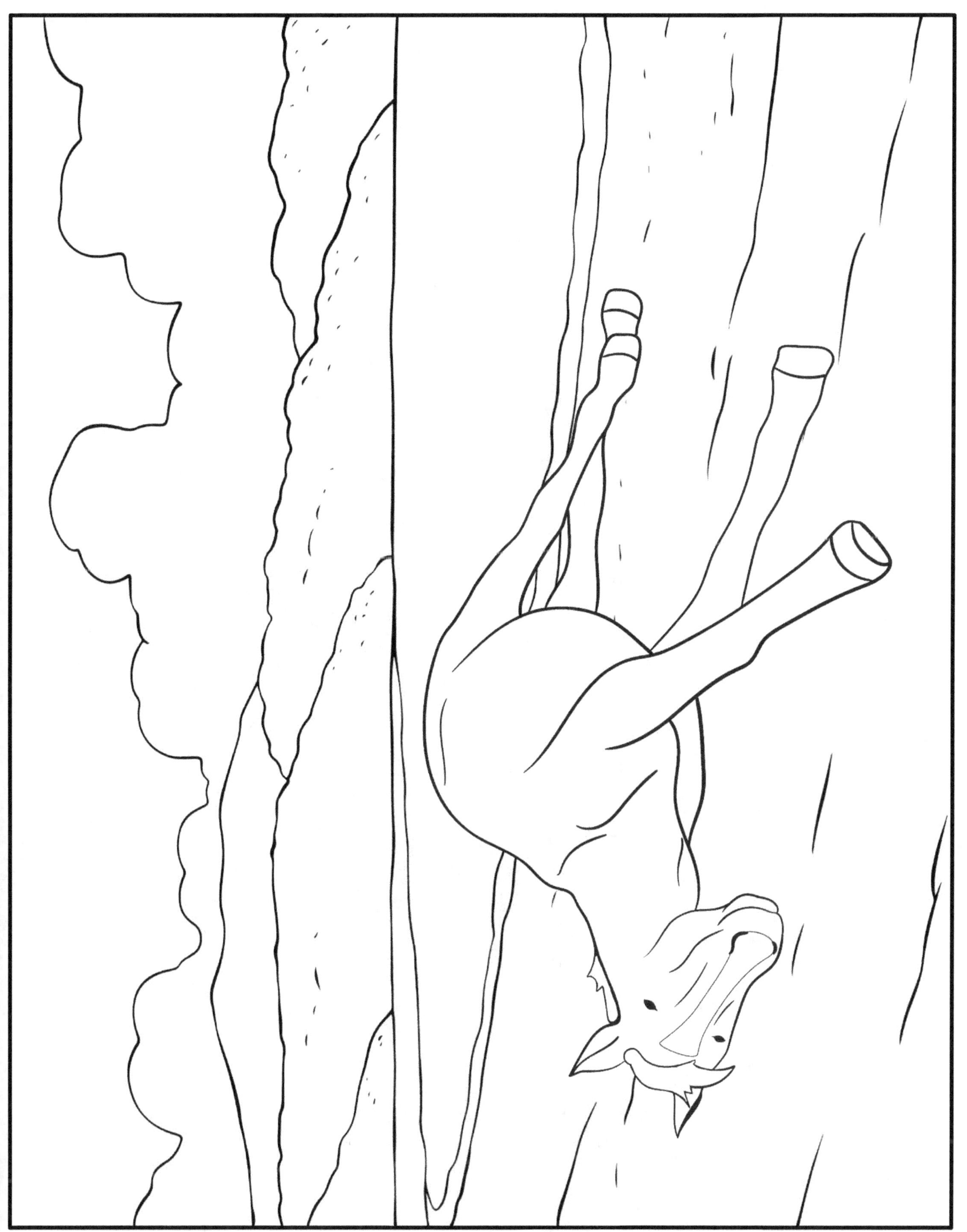

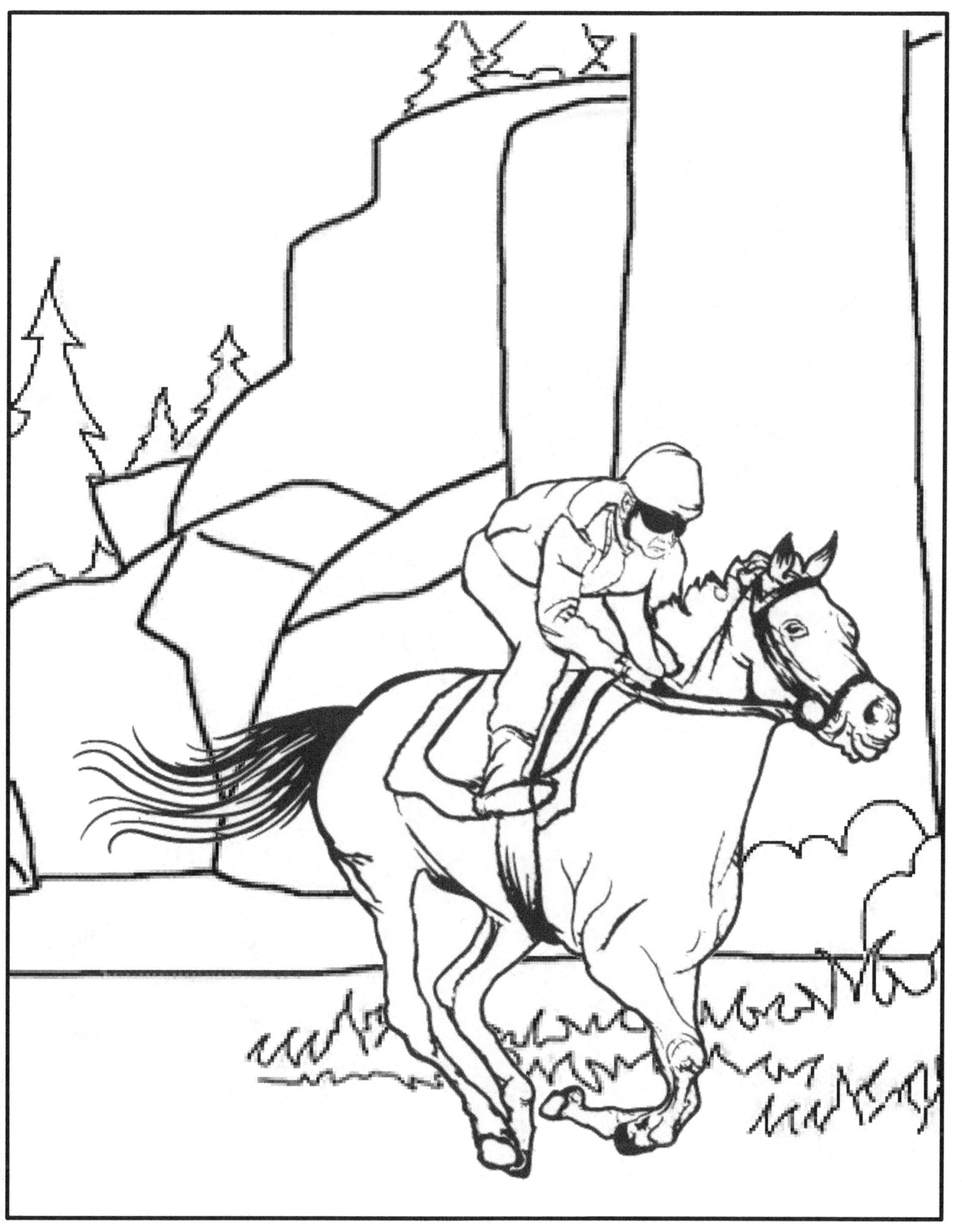

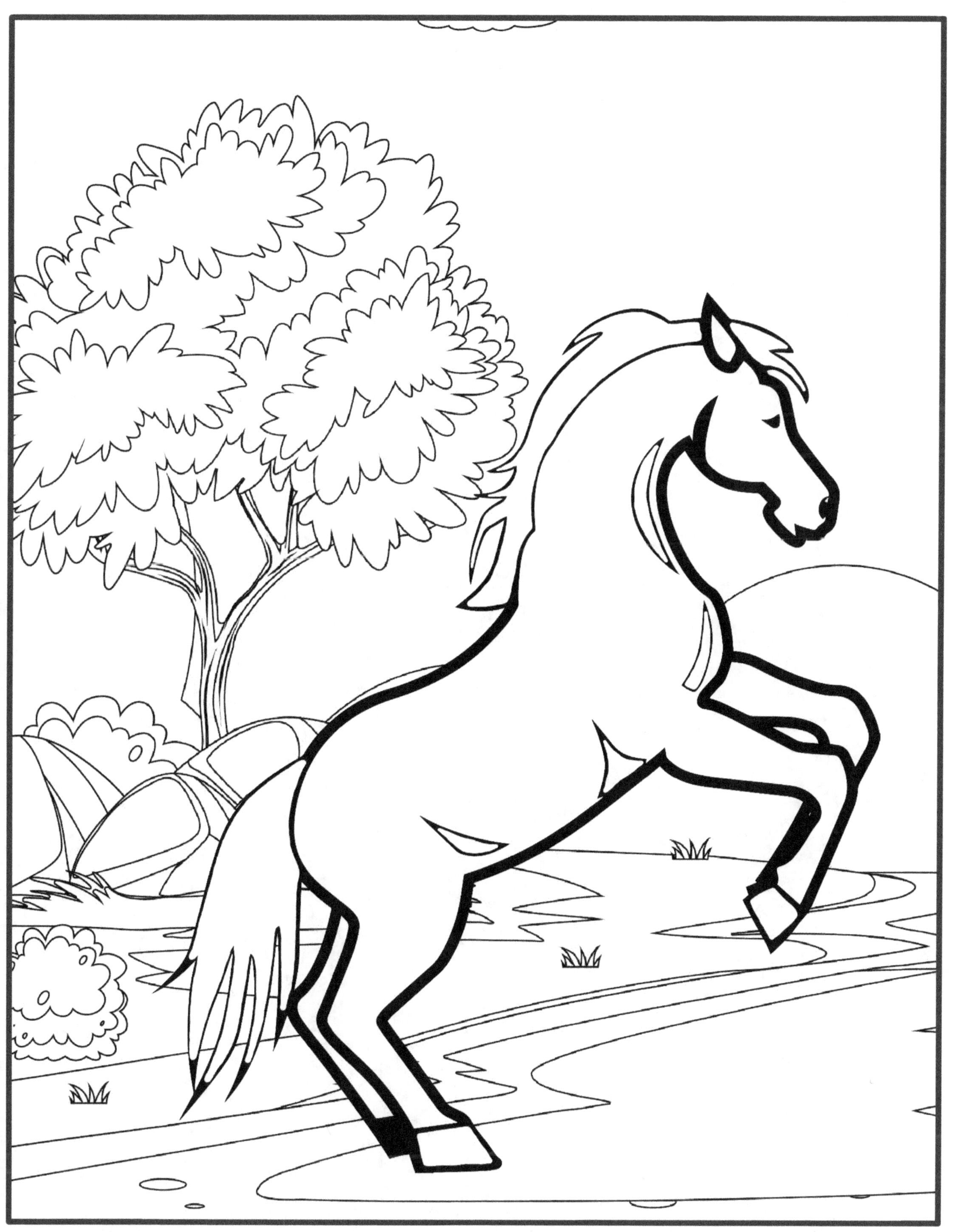

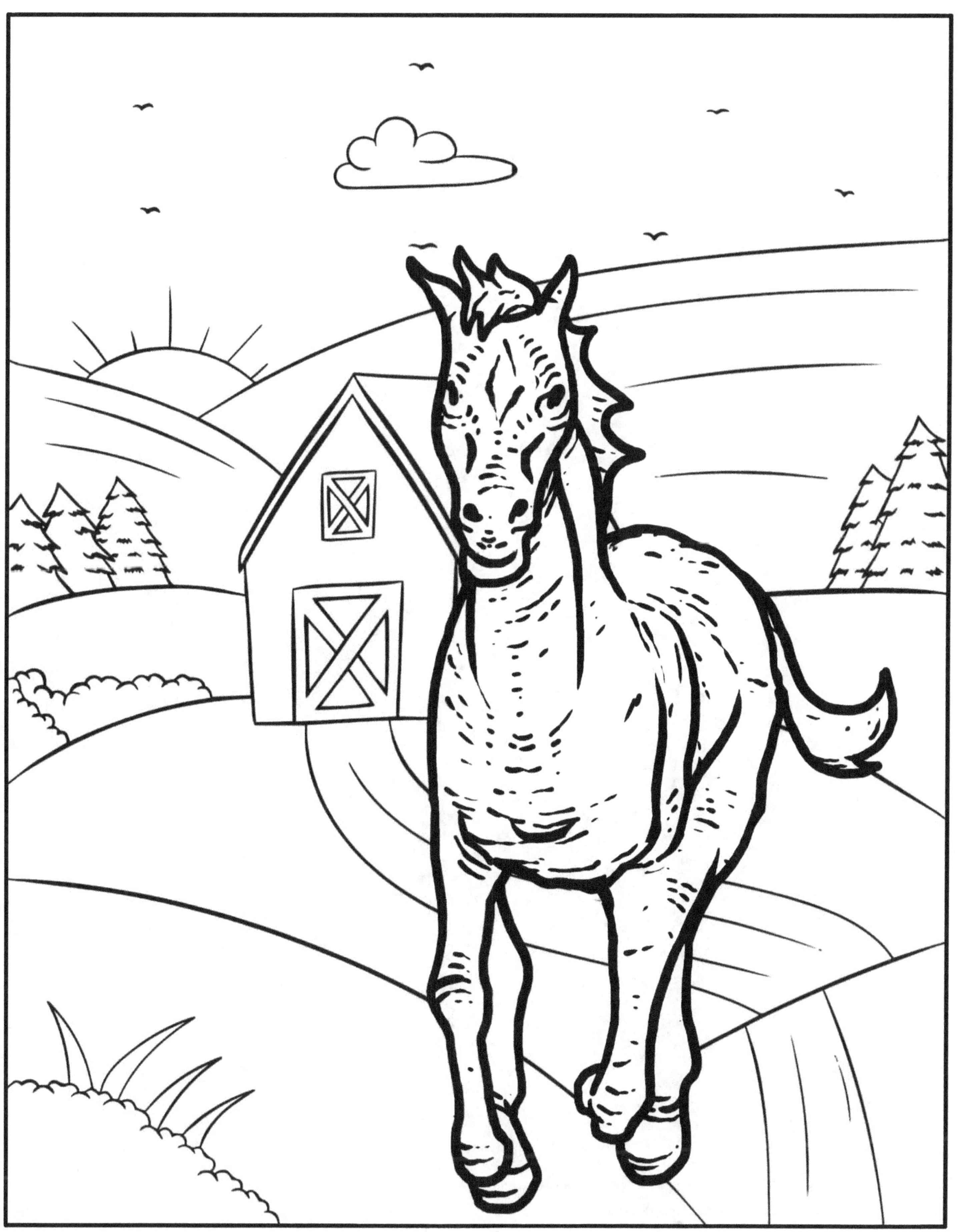

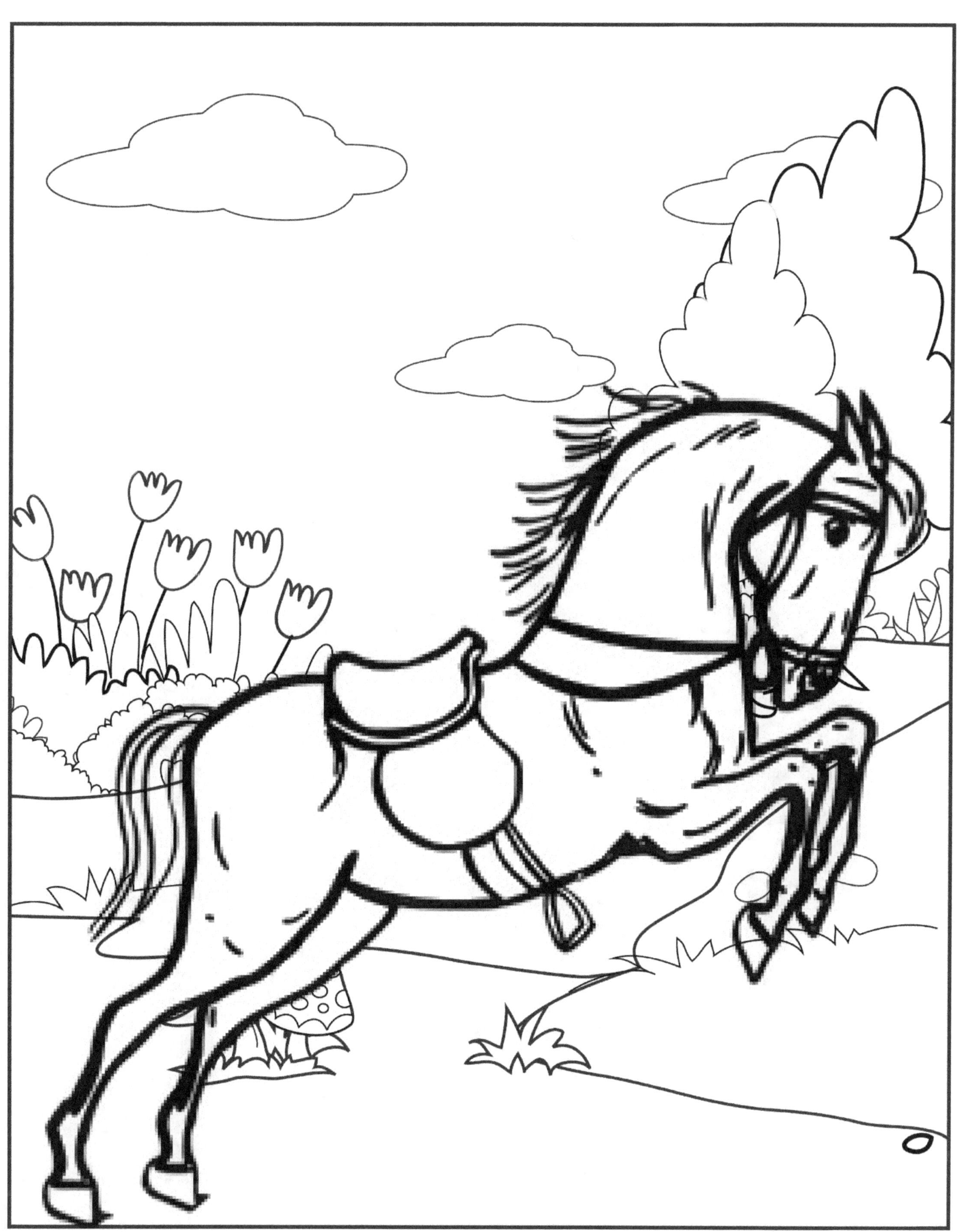

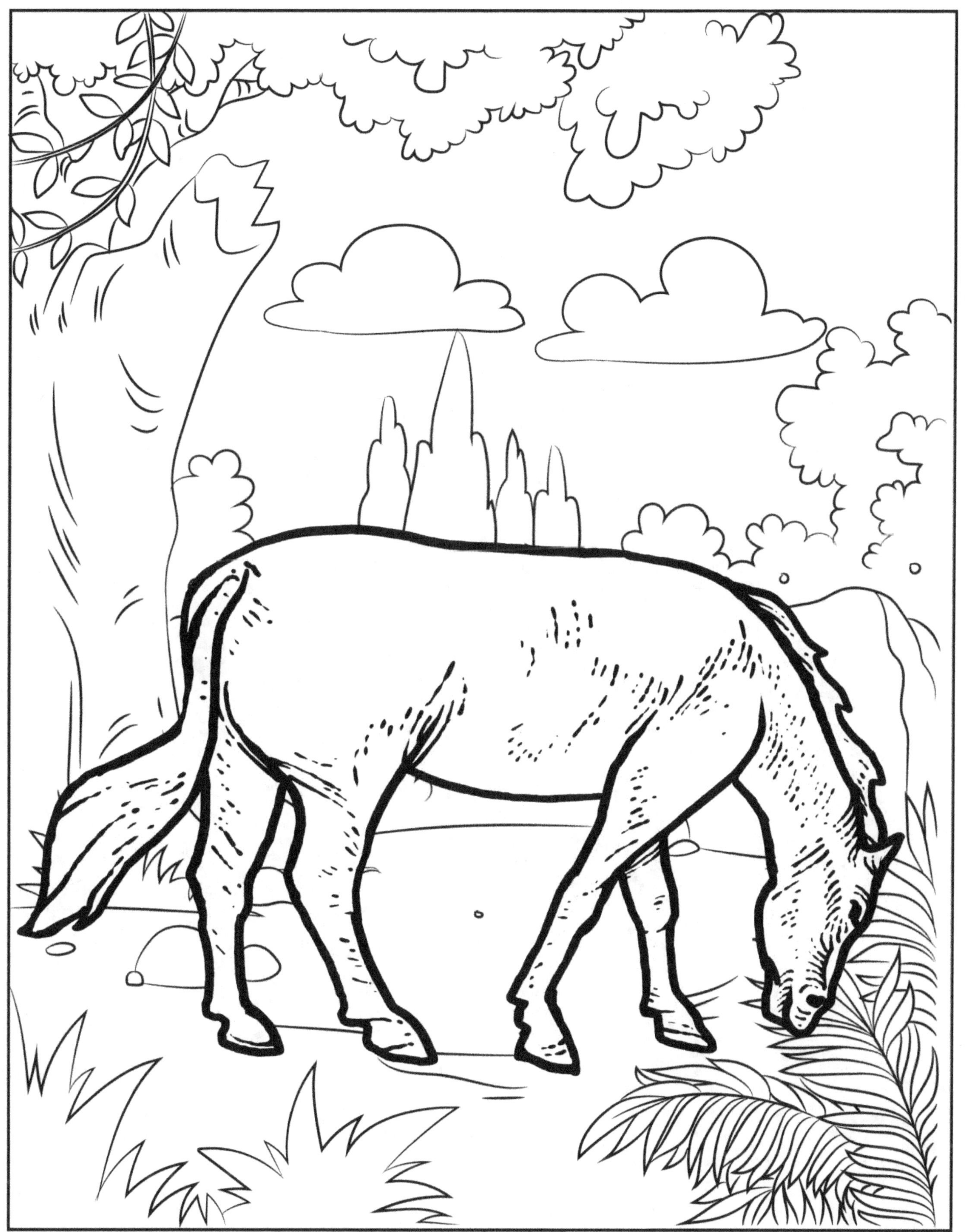

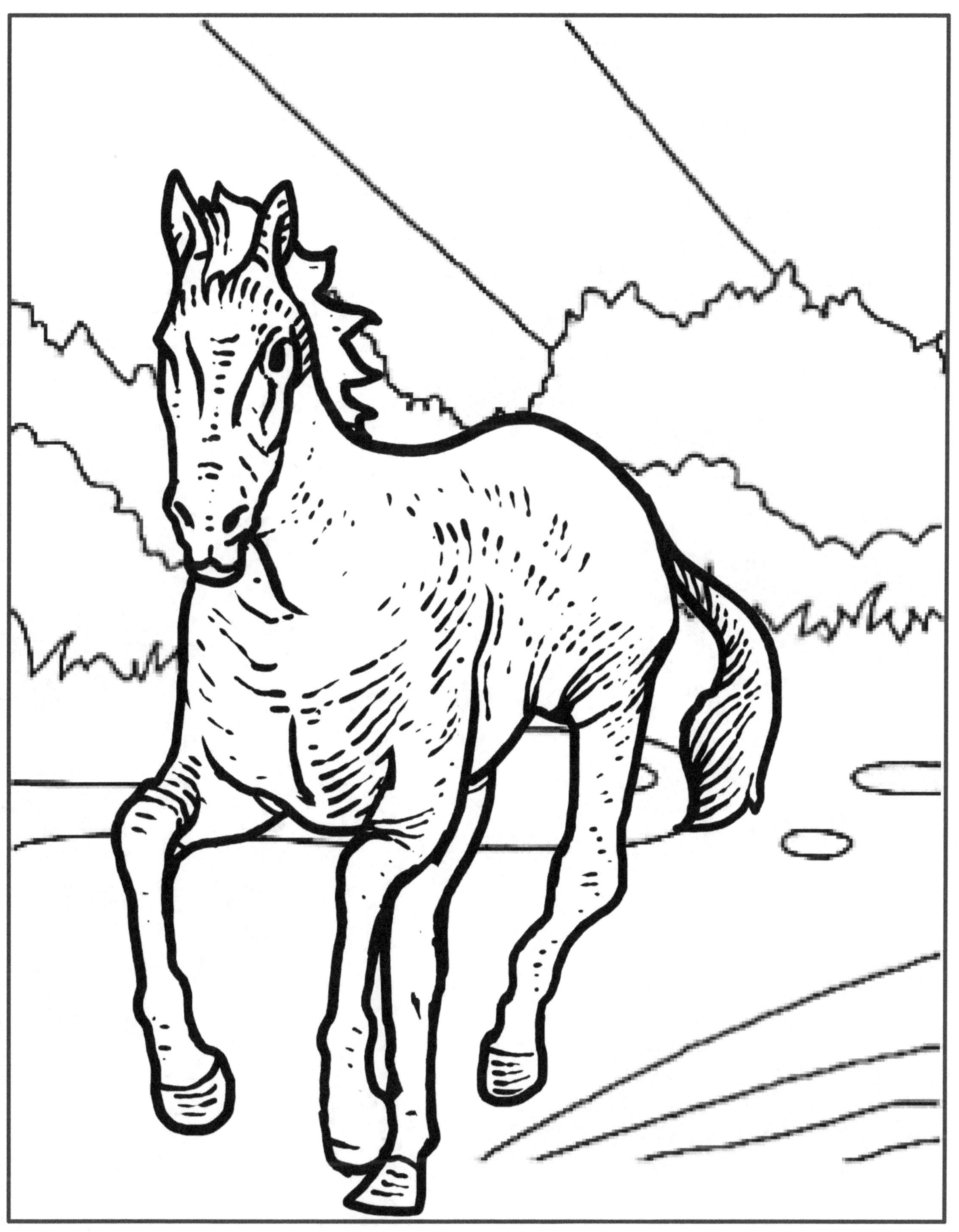